Always Choose To Be You!

Mark

PRAISE

The timing could not be any better for Mark Brown's "Choose To Be You", a genuine, heart-felt book about the struggle to find one's true self. These challenging times have made it even more difficult for us to live through our core selves...and avoid the daily temptations to make choices based on the opinions of others. Mark tells his humble, honest story of his teenage battles with self-esteem and how it ultimately shaped his now highly successful life as a husband, father and high school administrator. If you have ever felt "not good enough" in any way, this book will be a must-read for you!

Tom Cody
Author | Speaker with Top 20 Training

Choose To Be You lives up to the name! Mark does an epic job of challenging us all to really choose to be who we are, not who we're pretending to be! I straight up 10 outta 10 recommend this book!

Mike Smith
Founder of
Author | Misfit

When you meet Mark Brown you quickly realize that you are in the presence of a genuine, caring human being. When you hear him tell his story you realize that his honesty and openness are gifts that can't be measured. When you read this story, His story, you will realize that there is wisdom for everyone within its pages. Whether you are a student, an educator or someone just looking for inspiration, Mark's story is a story of hope and determination. He shines the light on the importance of relationships in all that we do and provides a road map for you to truly Choose To Be You.

Paul C. Dols
Climate and Culture Coordinator
Monrovia High School, Monrovia, CA
Renaissance Hall of Fame

Within Choose To Be You, Mark Brown provides us with a raw, unapologetic insight to the challenges of his life that shaped him into the educator and leader he is today. In turn, he provides key points to helping our own students who may be going through their trials and how the leaders in our schools can support and help them become the best versions of themselves, not from lack of challenges but by working through them.

Bradlee W. Skinner
Author | Educator | Entertainer

Mark Brown has opened his heart in order to move you forward in life. This book, Choose To Be You is more than sharing a few good ideas. It is an exploration into what many of us are feeling and living with and a guide to how to make the world a better place. This is a book you need to read again and again.

Steven Bollar aka Stand Tall Steve
Speaker | Trainer | Author
Renaissance Hall of Fame

As great as social media is to connect and collaborate with other educators, watching the highlight reel of others can cause imposter's syndrome or the guilt of feeling one doesn't measure up to some false narrative in their role. In Choose to Be You, Brown shares his personal story, offering the needed encouragement to just simply be who YOU are! As an educator, your fingerprints of impact are unique; with each imprint being personal and authentic. So, be proud. Be fearless. Be who you are meant to be!

Thomas C. Murray
Director of Innovation, Future Ready Schools ®
Best selling author of Personal & Authentic: Designing
Learning Experiences that Impact a Lifetime
Washington, D.C.

Honest. Raw. Inspiring. Mark shares his personal and authentic story as he seeks out the best version of himself in his book, Choose to Be You. His words are an inspiration to both educators, students, and any individual looking to find their way whether that be in life, leadership positions, or in the classroom. The connections he makes with the reader leaves them feeling as if they were right there with Mark as he shares his triumphs, challenges, and life lessons. Whatever is holding you back, choose to be you! #ChooseToBeYou

Dr. Rachael George
Principal | Author

Choose to be You is a compilation of reminders to live your WHY. Mark uses his personal stories to share with us a remarkable view into what it means to overcome adversity. His transparency is a model for us all on how to live life on purpose, using who we are at our core to positively influence those around us.

Bethany Hill
Educator | Administrator
Cabot, Arkansas

I love Mark's story!! Being authentic and vulnerable can be powerful and Mark is proof of that! Although still semi-young, Mark is building a great story, already has a great story to tell that is impactful, and will continue to build it for decades to come. Please take the time to read what Mark has to say and share about his own journey. It will bless you and will challenge you to be authentic, vulnerable, and want to leave a legacy.

Dr. Steve Woolf
Superintendent | Author
Renaissance Hall of Fame

In Choose to be You, Mark Brown displays the courage it takes to be honest as educators and human beings about mental health. His vulnerability is on full display in every single page of the book as he delves into the ups, the extreme downs, and everything in between of his life. I found myself in constant self-reflection about my own journey as an educator and was connecting with so many things that Mark said!

Brad Weinstein
Educator | Author | Speaker

Real, Honest, Insightful - In Choose to Be You, Mark Brown takes the reader on a journey that is not just his but could belong to any student in our classrooms and hallways. Mark opens his heart about his own struggles and how he has both overcome and applied them to his leadership journey supporting and honoring his students. This book needs to be your next educational read!!

Darrin M Peppard, Ed.D.
Superintendent | Author of Road To Awesome
Renaissance Hall of Fame

Choose To Be You is the call to live your life as your best version of yourself . Mark's story is one that is compelling, vulnerable, and inspiring. His journey of Choose to Be You makes you reflect not only on your impact as an educator but the impact you are having on yourself. This is a must read to start on your journey to become your most authentic self!

Melissa Wright
Educator, Kennebecasis Valley High School

Mark Brown's writing is vulnerable and compelling. As a school leader it can be easy to lose yourself when you are trying to be everything to everybody. Mark reminds us that our beauty lies in our humanity, and isn't until we fully embrace that humanity--imperfections and all--that we truly can be whole enough to lead and love bravely.

Dr. Amy Fast
Principal | Author | Education Commentator

Vulnerability alongside practicality is a recipe for meaningful change — for educators, students, and all of us. Mark Brown's Choose To Be You provides real life stories and powerful resources to help you find your voice and shape the world for the better.

Houston Kraft
Co-Founder of CharacterStrong | Author of Deep Kindness

I love this book! It has a timely message for students, leaders, educators and really anyone who wants to be a better version of themselves and create change around them. Mark is thought-provoking and insightful while being honest and vulnerable - you feel like you're sitting across from him sharing stories.

Sara Nilles
Executive Director Oregon Association of Student Councils
Educational Consultant for Work2BeWell

Compelling. Real. Must Read! Every day you have a choice. Mark's book allows you to have the courage to reflect upon who you are. His journey allows you to use your imperfections as a source of strength. Choose your path. Choose to Be You! Only read this book if you want to be inspired!

Dr. Frank Rudnesky
Retired Educator | Author | Speaker
Renaissance Hall of Fame

Wow! It's rare that we are given the gift from someone who is willing to reveal themselves in a way that we gain a sneak-peek into another human's life to see how our stories are vastly different...and similar. As Mark reveals layer after layer of human experiences and thoughts, one can't help but take a moment to reflect, consider and remind ourselves that we are all in this together, even when we feel alone!

LaVonna Roth
Creator of Ignite Your S.H.I.N.E.®
Speaker | Author | Chief Illuminator
igniteyourSHINE.com

CHOOSE
TO BE YOU

MARK BROWN

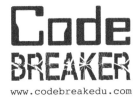

www.codebreakedu.com

This book is dedicated first to my wife, Sarah. Thank you for loving me, supporting me, encouraging me, and standing by me every step of the way. You have shown me the meaning of unconditional love and I would not be where I am today without you by my side. I love you, forever and always!

To my daughters, Addy and Rose. I love you and am so lucky to be your Dad! My hope and prayer for you is that you grow up and find confidence in who you are as individuals, and that you live your life choosing to be YOU!

To my parents, Craig and Mara Brown. Thank you for giving me the best life a kid could dream of having! Thank you for loving me and for always being there to catch me when I fell.

To everyone reading this, this book is for you. I hope you will find courage and strength to Choose To Be You. You deserve it and the world needs you to be YOU!

ACKNOWLEDGEMENTS

This book would have never happened without the help and support of several people who mean so much to me! There are countless individuals who have played a role in helping me become the person I am today and who have helped shape the story and message of *Choose To Be You*. To everyone who has walked alongside me, loved me, supported me, encouraged me, taught me, and modeled for me what it means to *Choose To Be You*, thank you!

Thank you to Dr. Phillip Campbell. You were one of the first people to believe in the power of the message of *Choose To Be You* and encouraged me to chase the opportunity to publish my story in order to positively impact others. Thank you for mentoring me and supporting me as an educator. But most of all, thank you for your friendship! I am beyond blessed to call you my friend!

Thank you to Dr. Darrin Peppard for helping me navigate and understand what it takes to publish a book and for connecting me with Brian and the Code Breaker family. Thank you for your constant encouragement and for showing me how to live life while traveling down the Road To Awesome!

Thank you to Brian Aspinall for taking a chance on me and giving me the opportunity to publish this book. I am humbled and blessed to be a part of the Code Breaker family and am thankful to be connected with you not only as my publisher, but as a mentor and a friend!

Thank you to Daphne McMenemy. You are amazing! Thank you for the countless hours you spent editing and working to bring the message of *Choose To Be You* to life! Thank you for all of the text messages, emails, and video calls to make sure everything was just right. This book, but more importantly the message of *Choose To Be You*, would not be what it is without you!

Thank you to all of the educators and coaches who have inspired me to be the best version of me in order to best support students. I am blessed to work with and be connected to so many amazingly talented and passionate educators. Thank you for inspiring me to be better and for working each and every day to positively impact the lives of others!

Thank you to my students and players. Thank you for allowing me the opportunity to teach and coach you. It is an absolute privilege and blessing to work with each and every one of you!

Thank you to my family: Dad, Mom, Joel, Erin, Margot, and Joy. I love you all!

Thank you to my daughters: Addy and Rose. Thank you for being you! You both inspire and challenge me to be better every single day. I love you!

Finally, thank you to my wife, Sarah. Thank you for all that you have sacrificed over the past 14 years in order to support me in pursuing my career as a teacher, administrator, and coach. Thank you for loving me even when I was not at my best. Thank you for choosing to walk through both the high and lows of life with me. Thank you for encouraging me to chase my dreams and for being my biggest advocate and cheerleader. Thank you for holding our family together and for loving me, Addy, and Rose unconditionally. I love you, forever and always!

TABLE OF CONTENTS

FOREWORD

Who are you, when the world's not looking?

We live in a society with a constant pressure to do more, to attain more, and to be more. From the clothes that we wear to the vehicle that we drive to the size of our home, there is a constant sense of comparison around what I have, or don't have, compared to those around us. And not even those simply in our physical proximity; social media has made our world of comparisons global in scale.

In a world full of stereotypes, it's interesting to consider *when* those stereotypical beliefs begin to take root. As I look back on pictures of myself from my early elementary school days, it is readily apparent that I was not at all concerned with my sense of fashion. By my early high school days, however, everything had to be perfect and on brand; from my shoes to my outfit to my necklace to my hair. Every detail mattered in an effort to be accepted by my peers.

One of the most difficult realities of my teenage years was when I got my first car. I didn't grow up poor by any stretch of the imagination, but I was far from being affluent either. Because of that, I had to wait until I was

17 years old to get my first car. With my parents' help, we paid $1,200 for a 1983 Subaru hatchback. It was white, it had cloth seats, and it was UGLY. Even worse, the brakes made an unbelievable screeching sound, which announced my presence in a neighborhood from miles away. Needless to say, nothing about this car was cool, and nothing about the reactions I received from other people on the road indicated that I was cool either.

Immediately after graduating from high school, I bought a new vehicle. I purchased a 1998 Jeep Wrangler. Hunter green, tan top, roll bar, jacked up tires…my Jeep was SWEET. And all of a sudden, *I was cool*…not only in my own mind, but through the looks I received from others on the road as well. Even though it was still the same exact person driving the Jeep who was driving the Subaru, for whatever reason, in my mind, it made people view me in a different light.

I first met Mark a few years back at a tour stop where I was speaking in his home state of Oregon. It didn't take me long to figure out that he would become a sacred member of my PLC. One of the most genuine and authentic people I know, Mark is the consummate "good guy" who is always supporting and cheering for others to be successful. In a world full of "me," Mark is the exception to the rule.

Through building our relationship, I have been blessed to have several impactful conversations with Mark. Through those conversations, I have learned that we have so much in common. We both love teaching. We both love kids. We both love sports. We both value relationships. And, we both have an underlying fear of not being accepted, of not measuring up, and of not being good enough for those around us.

Up until this point in time, it has largely been taboo to discuss mental health issues. More specifically, eating disorders in men have been almost unheard of. Because of this, many people, young and old alike, struggle with sharing their stories and seeking help for issues that society largely brands as weakness.

More and more, however, it is becoming acceptable to have a conversation around mental health. It is becoming acceptable to admit that you might not be perfect. It is becoming acceptable to be transparent with issues that you are struggling to fight against on your own. It is ok to not be ok.

It takes extreme courage to be vulnerable, to share your story, and to put yourself out there for the world to see...maybe not so much the good, but most definitely the bad and the ugly. But, it is through these difficult conversations that we inspire and empower others to share their stories and vulnerabilities as well.

It is important to understand that without adversity, there is no growth. Through the pages of this book, I hope that you will be encouraged to examine your personal viewpoints, not just towards others and the inherent stereotypes we all place through physical appearance and attributes, but of your own self-worth and value as well. Whether you are driving a 1983 Subaru or a 1998 Jeep, learn to be comfortable in your own skin, love yourself, and choose to be you.

Dr. Phillip Campbell
Author | Speaker
Jostens Renaissance Ambassador

PREFACE

*W*hat do you want to be when you grow up? This question is one that is commonly and almost routinely asked to young people beginning around the time they start to talk. In fact, my oldest daughter just turned four years old and I have already asked her this question multiple times. Typically, kids respond with fun and cute answers that make adults smile. Responses likely range from ladybug to firefighter to teacher and everything in between. If we were to do a research study, I imagine that the results would conclude that the majority of people do not enter into the professional field of their choice from when they were asked the question 'What do you want to be when you grow up' as kids.

So why do we ask this question so commonly and so often to kids? I can't tell you how many times I was asked that question growing up, or how many times I have asked that question to my students. For me, my answer to the question changed many times over the course of my childhood. Some of the changes were because my interests changed, but others were because I wanted to give an answer that people would approve of. I can remember that even at a young age, I felt like I was being judged when I was asked that question. I believed that I had to give the 'right' answer so that whoever was asking would approve of my dreams, goals, and aspirations for growing up to be what our society defined as a successful person.

Growing up, I had the best possible home life a kid could dream of having. My mom and dad loved and supported me unconditionally, and today, they are two of my best friends. They showed me the meaning of unconditional love by the way they loved each other and how they loved me and my two siblings. They had an amazing ability to know just how much space and freedom to give us at different stages of growing up so that we made our own path and made our own decisions, even if it meant making some mistakes, but they were always there to catch us when we fell and provided us with the guidance, love, and support we needed to get back on our feet. I did not always recognize or appreciate this at the time, but looking back, I am grateful for the experiences I had growing up. I am thankful that I learned some tough lessons along the way, but that I never had to go through any of it alone. Mom and Dad were always there to love me, to listen to me, and to provide the wisdom and guidance I needed to keep moving forward.

My dad was a full time preaching minister and my mom was a homemaker. I have an older brother, Joel, and a younger sister, Joy. We lived in a two-story house in a nice neighborhood. We ate dinner together around the table every night. My dad coached my brother and me in little league. We were basically the poster family for what had been described as the *American Dream*. We even had the dogs! Seriously, I'm not making this up. We had it all! We may not have been the most wealthy family and my parents worked hard to be creative in never letting us children feel as if we couldn't afford nice things, but they always made sure we had what we needed. Looking back on it, I realize that I was the

luckiest kid in the world! However, it took me over thirty years, and a lot of emotional scars to finally see it that way.

My siblings and I all went to a small private school across town from where we lived. It was a good school with caring teachers. From kindergarten through eighth-grade, our dad drove us to school in the mornings, and then we carpooled home after school with another family who lived on the same side of town as us. The major downside to living on the opposite side of town was that we rarely hung out with our school friends outside of the regular school day. When we got home, we weren't really connected with the kids in our neighborhood because they all went to public school together. Additionally, much of our free time was spent at the church building, which was also in a completely different part of town. We kinda had three worlds that we lived in: home, school, church.

In all three worlds, I felt like I had to be someone different. In all three worlds, I did whatever I needed to do to gain the approval of adults. In my mind, it didn't matter as much what my peers thought of me, as long as the adults liked me and approved of who I was as a person. I had perfect attendance, great grades, and zero behavioral referrals (until third grade, which we'll get to later). In fact, when I was in second grade, I got called to the principal's office and was scared out of my mind! I had absolutely no idea why I was being called in to meet with him! When I finally got there, I was told that they wanted to videotape me interacting with the principal for a promotional video they were making for the school. They wanted me to smile and have a conversation with him, and then even pretend like we were saying a prayer together for the video while we held hands across his desk. Again, I was the poster child! Everything about my life was perfect… or at least that's what I tricked myself, and eventually others, into believing. In fact, my entire mission in life was to live in a way that caught other people's attention and made them notice me. I lived to seek approval from others. I wanted to be noticed, and for other people to recognize that I had it all together. Every decision I made and every interaction I had was done strategically through the lens of making sure it would catch the attention of others, and that they would be impressed with my accomplishments. Although it was exhausting, it was also exhilarating, and I quickly became addicted to seeking attention, value, and approval from others.

This pattern and way of living did not stop in elementary school. In fact, this was only the beginning of a deep, dark, slippery path that I would slide down through high school, college, the beginning of my career as an educator and coach, and one that ultimately took complete control of my life. I was 31 years old before I was able to look in the mirror and truly examine my life, and accept the reflection of who I am. It didn't happen because I gained a hero's load of courage. It happened because I had finally had enough and because I could no longer go on living life chasing someone and something other than the real, authentic me.

If you are looking for an entertaining story and light read, this book is not for you. As you read this book, you will encounter the lowest of lows from my life, and learn about the issues and struggles of someone who spent their life hiding behind a mask, and who still wrestles daily with a heavy mental illness. You will be challenged to reflect on your own life and face your own challenges and struggles head on. You will be expected to take a stand and fight to *Choose To Be You,* while also fighting for those who might not yet be able to fight for themselves. To truly embrace the call and cry of *Choose To Be You*, we must find strength in who we are as individuals, but then extend that right to others by encouraging and allowing them to be who they are.

As life-long learners, our learning should be centered on who we are at our core. As educators, our primary responsibility is to love and empower learners to *Choose To Be You,* and provide learners with opportunities to be challenged to grow in unique ways. As humans, the key to living our best life is to live life exactly as who we are, unapologetically, and to love and support others in living their best life exactly as they are. My hope is that by sharing my story, you will be inspired, encouraged, and empowered to *Choose To Be You.*

This book is rooted in my personal story and is largely written as a memoir. I choose to openly share my story in hopes that you will find connections to your own life and experience. Some of the stories I share are fun while others are difficult to write about and read. Throughout the book, I share experiences and events that I still struggle to process and understand today. I want to be clear that I do not write any of this to place blame on any of the events or individuals who were involved in any of these experiences. The desire and need to place blame is not a part of my healing, and will do nothing to help me move forward today. These are simply stories that shaped who I am today, and that have impacted who I am choosing to be moving forward.

As you read, you will be offered the opportunity to interact with the reading and make *Gut Checks* to your life as either an individual or a learner, or to your work as an educator. Whenever you see *Gut Checks*, I encourage you to take the time to reflect, write, and apply what you've read to your life. Again, my hope in writing this book is not that you find it entertaining, but that you find it as a source of encouragement to help you *Choose To Be You,* so that you can be fully equipped in helping to support others in finding who they are and embracing the call to *Choose To Be You.*

GUT CHECK

What is the biggest barrier you face in your life that prevents you from embracing the call to *Choose To Be You?* Why is living your best life as your authentic self so challenging and difficult?

CHAPTER

ONE

THE POWER OF COOL PANTS

My first real experience with rejection happened in seventh-grade. I had become really good friends with several of the girls in my grade, and most of them were involved in theatre. I decided to audition for the school play. The theatre director was also one of my favorite teachers, so it was easy for me to say yes when asked by the girls to audition. Although I had never been in any type of play or theatre production before, besides the elementary Christmas pageant, I had my heart set on getting the lead role! I don't know why, but I just expected to waltz into auditions, wow everyone with my stage presence, and become an overnight star. Remember, I was addicted to seeking approval and value from others. In my mind, the only way to gain approval was by getting the lead role.

I had always been a good speaker and presenter, so I figured I had this in the bag! When the cast list was released, my heart sank when my name wasn't at the top. I was cast into a supporting role, and I was devastated. However, the worst was yet to come. The theatre director could tell that I was pretty bummed about not being cast as the lead, so she pulled me aside and tried to explain to me why I wasn't selected for the role I had so desperately wanted. Although she had the best of intentions, and I still respect her as one of my favorite educators of all time, what she said to me crushed me. She told me that one of the main reasons I was not cast as the lead was because I was too short and it wouldn't look right for me to be shorter than the lead female. I'm sure that she said other reasons, but that was all I heard. I was crushed. Unfortunately, this put the idea in my head that my appearance played a major role in my success, and that people were going to judge me for the rest of my life based on how I looked. I suddenly became hyper-aware of my appearance. As someone who is addicted to seeking value and approval from others, once you know what it is about yourself that others don't like or approve of, you cannot stop thinking about it and it controls almost every single thought you have about yourself. From that point forward, I started to notice everything that was wrong with my appearance and became ashamed of the image I saw in the mirror. I started to connect all of my failures in life to my body image.

The rejection I experienced in seventh-grade was not the first time in my life that I noticed I was different from most people in regards to my physical appearance and size. Growing up, I was ridiculously small. Not just a little shorter and skinnier than everyone else, but super small for my age! I remember playing t-ball and getting my first pair of baseball pants. They were so small that even the elastic around the waist wasn't tight enough to keep my pants from falling down.

My mom, being the supermom that she is, sewed belt loops onto the pants so that I could wear a belt to keep my pants from falling down. She did an amazing job of convincing me that these were "cool" pants so that I didn't feel singled out for having pants that were different from everyone else. My mom could not control the fact that the pants did not fit me. She could not control the fact that she had to visibly alter the pants from their original state in order for them to be wearable during games. She was however, able to control how she influenced my feelings about the pants by the way she talked about them. Instead of blaming my small stature for the reason my pants were different, she was creative in being excited as she talked about how cool and special my pants were. She made it seem like a big deal that I was able to wear a belt, because only big kids pants had belt loops. Instead of being

embarrassed that I was wearing pants that were different from everyone else, I was convinced and believed that I was wearing the cool pants!

GUT CHECK

As an **individual**, when was a time in life that you felt special, and like you were the one wearing the cool pants? Who was responsible for helping you feel that way?

As a **learner**, did you ever have an educator who went out of their way to make you feel special? If so, have you let that educator know how much you appreciate them and how much of an impact they had on your life? If you haven't, I strongly encourage you to do so. Hearing from past students about the impact we had on them as an educator is one of the most rewarding and fulfilling parts of our job!

As an **educator**, what can you do to help students feel like they are the ones wearing the cool pants, especially when they might be struggling or when they might see their differences from others as a bad thing?

In my early years of school, I was always friends with most everyone in my class. I was the kid who could bounce from one group to another, and not miss a beat. However, as I moved into upper-grade school and early middle school, things started to change. As we got older, there was much more of an emphasis and focus on sports. One's popularity was directly correlated to your athletic ability or skill. I had always been decent at sports. I was never the best, but I could compete in most sports and hold my own. However, as I got older, sports became more and more difficult for me.

Growing up, I was given medication for complications with my asthma. At the time, we didn't know the risks associated with being on this specific medication. However, today we know that there can be delayed side-effects, one of which is drastic weight change and damage to the metabolic system. After being on and off medication for more than three years, my body started changing around the time I was in third-grade. I began gaining weight but didn't grow in height at a consistent rate. I went from being the super skinny, short kid to the super chubby, short kid. I put on a lot of weight, quickly.

I should probably mention that I didn't have the best eating habits. Nearly every day after school there were fresh cookies and milk waiting for me. If you know my mom, you know that she is famous for her cookies. To this day, when she comes to visit, she almost always arrives with a plate of fresh cookies in hand. Even more than just cookies, she is without a doubt the best cook in the whole world! The problem was that I had little to no control when it came to food.

I really started to recognize the impact of my weight gain as I got into middle school. I was still very active in multiple sports and loved competing. Although I still had the basic skills to compete, I was unable to keep up with the athleticism and speed of my peers. In middle school, the coolest kids in my grade all played basketball. I played in sixth-grade, but hardly got any playing time, and was often made fun of by my teammates because I couldn't keep up in practices. Once seventh-grade rolled around, I decided I was not going to play basketball. That was a really painful decision for me because it was almost as if I were officially not one of the cool kids.

Lucky for me, my principal knew me well enough to know that this was a difficult decision for me and that even though I had made the decision for myself that I was not going to play basketball, that I still needed some way of staying connected to the team. He offered me the opportunity to run the score clock during home games. He even said I could get paid for it! This was perfect! I would get to still be around the basketball team, and I would be making money! I had a blast that season! It definitely wasn't the same as being on the team, but it was all that I needed to still feel like I wasn't an outcast, and it came without the risk of embarrassing myself because I wasn't good enough to compete on the court.

I'll never forget the opportunity my principal extended to me that season. In fact, I would keep it with me and use it later in my life when I became a head basketball coach. Becoming a varsity basketball coach at a 6A high school, which is the largest division in the state of Oregon, was something I never dreamed of doing. As you'll continue to hear as you keep reading, I have never been the best on the basketball court. However,

I've always had a love for the game, and have wanted to somehow be connected to it. If you told any of my middle school or high school teammates that I would go on to become a 6A varsity head coach, they would have all laughed and called you crazy. However, because I have a passion for the game and had people in my life who gave me opportunities to be involved with the game, I achieved my dream of becoming a coach.

Each season, there are students who are either not able to play because of circumstances outside of their control, or they don't make the team because they do not have the skill. Making cuts is always the worst day of the year for me, and something I dread. Having to look a student in the eyes and tell them that they do not get to play basketball, something that they wanted so badly to do, is a terrible feeling. It literally drains every ounce of energy from your body and soul. However, because of the experience that my middle school principal gave me to still be involved, I've looked for ways to find opportunities for some of the students to still be involved with the basketball program as either a program assistant, filmer, or statistician. Again, in a perfect world, there would be a spot for everyone that tried out, but that is unfortunately not the case.

I have had some great help over the years, but one that made a tremendous impact not only on our basketball team, but also on my life personally was our Japanese foreign exchange student, Tomo. Although we were not able to offer Tomo a roster spot, I quickly noticed there was something special about Tomo. He was extremely friendly, and all of the players loved having him around. So, I asked Tomo if he would still like to be involved as a program assistant and help us out during the basketball season. He was excited about the opportunity and said yes!

Giving Tomo that opportunity was one of the best decisions I have ever made as a head coach. He was early to every practice and game to make sure that everything was ready for the players and the coaching staff. Even things that I or the other coaches had normally done to prepare for practices and games, he was taking it upon himself to manage. Being an exchange student, he was still working on his spoken English skills. During the first few practices, he struggled to understand when I would yell across the gym for him to put the time on the clock for a specific drill, or when I wanted him to keep score during a section of the practice. If you have ever worked a score clock, you know how confusing they can be with all of the various buttons and symbols, even if you are proficient in the language it is written in. But, on his own initiative, Tomo created a cheat sheet that helped him translate the buttons on the score clock from English into Japanese, so that he was quicker and more efficient in operating the clock. He was an amazing program assistant and a great addition to the team!

My favorite memory about Tomo came in our last regular-season game. It was a home game, so it was our Senior Night where we honored the seniors and their families. In the days leading up to the game, our Senior players came to me and asked if we could give Tomo a jersey so that he could dress down for Senior Night. I told them that I had to check with our Athletic Director to make sure that it was legal. I got the go-ahead but decided I wanted to make it a big surprise. As I headed into the locker room for our pregame talk, I had an extra jersey in a bag. I walked in, pulled out the jersey, and handed it to Tomo. The locker room erupted and everyone ambushed Tomo with hugs and high fives! Tomo was in tears and excitedly raced to put on the jersey.

It was a great game, because not only was it Senior Night, but we were playing our biggest rivals. The gym was packed! Going into the game, I wasn't sure when and if I was going to be able to get Tomo some playing time, because we needed to win the game in order to secure 2nd place in the league, and help our ranking for the state playoffs as much as possible. By the 4th quarter, we were up by about 15 points with two minutes left in the game. I had begun subbing some of our younger players into the game, and finally turned to Tomo and told him to check-in. As he got off the bench and walked to the scorer's table, everyone in the gym started cheering and got on their feet. They were all excited to see him get into the game!

As Tomo checked in, I called timeout and we drew up a simple play to get him a shot. On our first offensive possession, Tomo caught the ball exactly where we wanted him to catch it, but he missed the shot! Then, on our next possession, we ran the same action, got him the ball, and as he went to shoot, he got fouled. He was going to get two free throws! Even though we had the game won by this point, there was more excitement and intensity in the gym than there had

been all season long! Tomo stepped to the line for his first free throw... miss. As he stepped to the line for his second free throw, there was absolute silence throughout the gym. It was almost like a movie. As he released the ball on his shot, it almost felt like slow motion as we all

watched the ball fly towards the hoop.... SWISH!!!!

The gym erupted! The final buzzer sounded and our entire team stormed the court to huddle around Tomo! As a coach, there are only a few times when I have been as proud as I was at that moment. At that moment, our team and our school's excitement was not about winning the game, even though we had just beat our biggest rival and secured a 2nd place finish in our league and a guaranteed bid to the state tournament. Our shared excitement and joy were all because Tomo had his shining moment!

As educators and as adults, how we talk to youth and to students is something that we need to be very intentional about. It is impossible to give everyone what they want. There are a lot of lessons that can be learned through experiencing difficult situations like not getting the role in the play that we want or getting cut from the team. It is a great opportunity to help students learn how to be resilient and overcome challenges with a positive attitude, but a lot of it has to do with the words we use and what we can do to shine light on the student's strengths as opposed to only focusing on their weaknesses. I have not always been successful in having these difficult conversations with students, but my experience with my middle school principal and then with Tomo, along with understanding what my mom did to make me believe I was wearing the Cool Pants are a good reminder that the words we use when talking with students are powerful and can have a much bigger and long lasting impact than we realize.

GUT CHECK

As an **individual**, has there ever been a time when you went out of your way to advocate for someone else, the same way that my players advocated for giving Tomo an opportunity to dress down in our last game?

As a **learner**, how does it feel when others celebrate your success like my players celebrated the success of Tomo? How can you be sure to go out of your way to celebrate the successes of other learners?

As an **educator**, how can you make sure to provide learners with opportunities to be involved in something that they are passionate about, even if it means creating an opportunity that doesn't naturally exist?

CHAPTER

TWO

CONTROL THE
CONTROLLABLES

*P*art of my story is learning to not blame my situation or the challenges I face on things outside of my control. In order to *Choose To Be You*, we must take responsibility for our mistakes or our situation in life, and stop making excuses for ourselves based on things that are outside of our control.

In life, I believe we can control three things: Our Attitude, Our Effort, and How We Treat Others.

This is a big part of what it means to *Choose To Be You* and something I still intentionally work on.

As my body started changing, my self-confidence and self-concept also began to change. In first- and second-grade, I was able to represent my school in the district track meet as a member of the 4x100 relay team. As a little guy, I was speedy and quick. However, after having gained weight, I wasn't the fastest in the class anymore. I remember during tryouts for the relay team in third-grade, as soon as the race started, I intentionally stumbled and fell out of the starting blocks, being unable to complete the race. Rather than face the disappointment of not making the team, I felt it was a better option to not even give myself the chance by faking a fall and disqualifying myself from the competition. This was the first time that my *effort*, and specifically my intentional *effort* to not give my best *effort* in order to give myself an excuse, got in the way of me being true to who I am.

Aside from my body changing, my *attitude* also started to change. I remember third-grade being the first time in my educational career that I got 'in trouble.' My teacher had a card system for tracking behavior. I'm sure almost all of us remember the classroom management system of everyone starting with a green card, then if you got caught doing something wrong, you had to change your card to yellow as a warning. Then, if you were caught again, the card changed to red and that was bad news!

One day, during a group activity, I was working with some classmates who didn't agree with how I wanted to approach the project. In all honesty, I don't remember the specific details about what the project was, or what the argument was even about, but I definitely remember the outcome. After going back and forth about ideas, the others weren't budging, and I was becoming irritated. I finally had enough and I told one of my partners to shut up! At that exact moment, our teacher was making her rounds and had walked up behind me. She told me to go change my card. I could not believe it! This had never happened to me! As I slowly walked over to the board to change my card, I felt like the weight of the world and all eyes in the room were on me. Suddenly, I was one of "those" kids! You know, one of the kids that got in trouble. It was probably the most embarrassing moment of my life up to that point. My perfect streak of being the good kid had come to an end! Third-grade me felt that my life, as I knew it, would never be the same!

For the rest of the day, I was drowning in shame and self-disappointment. Luckily, my teacher noticed how hard I was taking it, and at the end of class, she asked me to stay back and talk with her. As soon as all of my classmates had left the room, she knelt down beside me and I immediately burst into tears and began apologizing. I was hoping that if I could get the first word in, it would soften the blow of her anger and wrath! But, to my surprise, she responded in a way that I will never forget. She put her hand on my shoulder and said the most amazing words: "It's alright, Mark. Mistakes happen." I could not believe it! She wasn't mad. In fact, she was being super kind and trying to make me feel better, rather than telling me how disappointed she was and reminding me of how badly I had messed up. I was not only relieved, but I was also amazed that she was not taking the opportunity to teach me a lesson through punishment. Instead, she took the opportunity to make it a teachable moment and reassured me that my past actions did not define who I am moving forward. She talked with me about how I needed to own up to my mistake, but that moving forward, I could overcome the mistake by apologizing to my classmate, and then make sure that I used this as a learning experience of how to recognize when I'm getting angry or frustrated, and that I need to find a healthier outlet than yelling and being disrespectful to others. She helped me understand that at that point, I could not control what had already happened. But, that I did have the opportunity and the power to control how I would respond moving forward. I will never forget her kindness, gentleness, and the grace that she extended to me through this experience. This was a great learning opportunity for me to begin to understand the power of *how we treat others.*

I have tried to incorporate this into my work as an educator. As a young educator, I tried to do everything by the book. My response to student behavior was to do whatever the student handbook said. I was like a robot when dealing with student behavioral situations. However, over the years, I learned that instead of reacting based on what was written in the handbook and assigning whatever punishment was listed for that type of infraction, it was more effective to approach the situation like my third-grade teacher did. I started having more direct follow-up conversations with students. I not only softened my approach to the situation, but I began giving students the opportunity to talk and explain what was going on in their life, or what led them to make the decision they did. It became a powerful practice of not only trying to change behaviors, but in building relationships with students. By looking at every discipline issue as a teachable moment with students, I was able to have a much greater impact on changing their behavior long term. By giving my students a listening ear and helping them process through their mistakes, they gained respect for me, and were able to learn through the situation as opposed to just serving their punishment and moving on. It was incredible! The number of referrals I wrote reduced to almost none. Behavioral issues in my classes decreased significantly. Once I started showing respect to students and met them on their level, they showed me respect and were more engaged as learners because they knew I cared about them as more than just students, but as individuals and who they are.

This approach has also been huge in my work as an administrator, but most importantly, it has helped me in learning how to be a father. Being a Dad is the hardest and best job in the world. It is also extremely intimidating and exhausting! I'll never forget that moment when I first held my oldest daughter, Addy, in my arms in the hospital room. The feelings of joy and happiness were overwhelming! More than that, as I held her and looked down at her, in an instant I finally understood and realized the responsibility I had in being her Dad. My wife, Sarah, and I had a responsibility to love and protect her, but we also had the responsibility to raise her and help her discover who she is as an individual. Our number one responsibility is to love her and support her in making the daily choice to be the best version of herself.

Now having two daughters, both Addy and Rose are my greatest sense of pride and joy! It doesn't mean that everyday raising them is easy. As any parent knows, raising children is the most exhausting thing you will ever do! But, the type of exhaustion changes as they grow. In the early years, it is physically exhausting because you are responsible for their every basic need. As they get older, the exhaustion becomes more about the emotional energy and the mental attention it takes to be a parent. Even though my daughters are still relatively young, I am beginning to understand this more and more every day. What I am learning is that it is easy to parent if I do it from the role of authoritarian. As a parent, my daughters understand that I am the boss, or at least that I can be if I want to. When they do something wrong, it is easy to shame them into correcting their behavior. When I want or need them to do something, it is easy to bark orders and force them to do it, even if they do not understand the why behind being forced to carry out the order or action. But what does that teach them and how does that help them later in life when they are going to have to be independent and make responsible decisions for themselves? As their dad, it is my responsibility to walk alongside them and facilitate learning opportunities for them each and every day. This is where parenting becomes absolutely exhausting, but this is where I, as a parent, have an opportunity to set my daughters up for long term success. When they misbehave or make mistakes, I have to intentionally choose how I am going to respond to them as either the authoritarian and disciplinarian, or if I am going to take the time to make it a teachable moment to help them understand that there are consequences for the decisions we make, but that we can learn through our mistakes to become better as individuals moving forward. When I ask them to do something, instead of simply barking

orders, I need to take the time to explain to them why we must carry out whatever the task is, and then work alongside them to complete it. By providing support, wisdom, and a ton of grace to Addy and Rose, they are learning how to be who they are. When they mess up, I need to hold them accountable. I also need to love and support them. When they are working hard to accomplish a task, I need to let them work independently, and provide whatever supports and resources I can to support them. This is not easy but this is helping set them up for a life of success in being able to be confident in embracing the call to *Choose To Be You.*

GUT CHECK

As an **individual**, when was a time that you needed kindness or grace, and it was extended to you by someone else?

As a **learner**, when you make a mistake, does the response of the educator impact your learning and the outcome of the experience?

As an **educator**, how do you respond to students when they mess up and make mistakes? Do you shame them, or do you love them, and use it as a teachable moment? Can you think of a specific time when you successfully turned a student's mistake into a teachable moment, and your relationship with that student was strengthened through the experience?

THREE

THE VALUE OF A CRUSHED PENNY

As my seventh-grade year went on, I became extremely self-conscious about my height, my weight, and my overall physical appearance. My classmates decided to start calling me *Bertha*. I'm still not exactly sure where the nickname originated from or why it stuck, but it definitely stuck! Everyone in my class referred to me as Bertha. I still have old yearbooks where people referred to me as Bertha when they signed it at the end of the year. The name really bothered me. I hated it, but in a weird way, it also made me feel somewhat connected and accepted by my classmates. So, instead of fighting it, I embraced it and acted as if I loved it. However, even though on the outside I appeared to accept and enjoy the nickname, I deeply despised it and began to distance myself from having any true friendships at school. During my seventh- and eighth-grade years, I didn't go to anyone's house and chose not to go to any after school activities, because I had no desire to hang out with my classmates. I petitioned my parents to let me switch schools, but it just wasn't possible at that point in time. By the end of eighth-grade, I didn't even want to attend my graduation. I went to appease my parents, but once the ceremony was over, I wanted nothing more than to walk out the door of that school and never look back. I had been there since preschool, having spent the last eleven years with the same people, and now wanted nothing to do with anyone there.

Outside of school, I became an arrogant jerk. Although people at church were always kind to me, I did whatever I could to posture myself to appear better and superior to others. I pushed some of my best and lifelong friends away, fearing that they too would hurt me if I let them remain close to me. I began to gravitate towards adults and kept a distance between myself and my peers. I chose to not be involved in the youth group or other events and activities unless I was given the opportunity to connect and interact with adults. Deep down, I realize now that I was doing whatever I could to subconsciously bypass highschool and pretend that I was already an adult. People often joked and commented about me being much older than my age, and I can recognize now that it was fairly obvious that I was working extremely hard to position myself as an adult, and not as a teenager because being a teenager was too painful.

Distancing myself from others and building barriers around my heart is something that I still struggle with today. Because of the relationship and friendship pain I experienced early on as a middle school student, I did whatever I could to protect myself from experiencing that same type of pain and disappointment at later points in life. I always had 'friends', but I had very few deep, intimate friendships. Even with my family, I kept an emotional distance and made sure to always have protective measures in place when things were difficult.

In fact, I recently had a conversation with one of my closest friends and people who I respect most in the whole world. He actually called me out, in a very loving and respectful way, for the fact that I had recently become more distant and closed off in our relationship. He pointed out that throughout interactions over the past year, I had caused him to assume and wonder if he had done something to hurt or offend me because I was not as kind and open with him as I normally was. He helped me realize that this is something that I still struggle with today. Letting people into my life is not easy. I am always fearful of being hurt when I make myself vulnerable. As was evident in this situation with my friend, as my relationships grow, my natural response is to regress when I feel that we are getting too close, because I want to subconsciously avoid the pain and rejection that I assume is coming. I am extremely thankful to my friend for helping me process through this, and I use these experiences as a reminder that vulnerability and relationship building is not easy, but that it is in our vulnerability that we can experience the full joy of meaningful relationships and connections with others.

We are hardwired for connection with other people.

Being in relationships is not just something we should do, it is something we need in order to function as healthy people.

It was not until I was 29 years old and at the Jostens Renaissance National Conference (JRNC) that I finally understood the importance and power of connection. It was my first year at JRNC and I was hooked on what they had to offer from a school climate and culture standpoint. I started making connections with educators across North America, and I felt like I had finally found other educators like me, who believed in what I believed in! It was awesome!

The importance and power of connection smacked me in the face on the night that everyone from the conference went to Disney World. I had never been. I was so excited to get to experience the happiest place on earth! As we loaded the busses, it was chaotic and nearly impossible to find any of the people that I had connected with earlier during the conference. I was the only person from my school there, so I ended up loading a bus by myself and was off to explore Disney World on my own. As we arrived at the park, I was in awe, gawking like a little kid at the rides and attractions. After riding a few rides, I realized I wasn't really having any fun. After only an hour or so in the park, I was ready to go back to the hotel. I was literally standing in the middle of Main Street USA, at the happiest place on earth, and all I wanted to do was to be anywhere but there. I was really missing my family. I decided to stop in the gift shop to purchase gifts for my girls. As I went to exit the shop, I saw one of those crushed penny machines. I put my fifty-one cents into the machine so I could take home a crushed penny to keep as a souvenir of my visit to Disney World.

As I rode the shuttle bus back to the hotel, I held that crushed penny in my hand and reflected on my visit to what was supposed to be the happiest place on earth. Some people spend an entire week exploring Disney, and I didn't last more than a few hours. I realized exactly what was missing: someone to share the joy and excitement with. I was all alone, and I was miserable. For someone who had spent so much of life pushing people away and building barriers to keep people out of my life, I was used to being alone. However, I could not ignore the fact that being alone made life miserable that day, and it took a trip to the happiest place on earth to make me realize how much better life is when we share and experience it with others.

Ever since my visit to Disney World, I now carry that crushed penny in my pocket every single day. I use it as a reminder to invest in relationships and that life is so much better when it is shared and experienced with others. I am reminded that even when it's difficult and  forces me to be vulnerable, it's way better to be connected with and in meaningful relationships with others.

The transition to investing deeply and intimately in relationships has not been easy. Having had spent the last fifteen years distancing myself from others, it has definitely been an adjustment to slowly break down those barriers and allow people into my life, and to share intimate experiences and information about who I am. As difficult and painful as it may seem initially, I am always encouraged at how much more joy I find in sharing life with others. This has helped me be a better husband and father. It has helped me be a better son and brother, as well as a coach and educator.

In schools, relationships must be at the core of everything we do.

Yes, we have a responsibility to provide a guaranteed and rigorous curriculum and academic experience for our students, but I am a firm believer that we will never be capable of living up to these expectations if we do not first and foremost focus on relationships. Every success we have in school is rooted in relationships. The emphasis on relationships and connectivity must be driven, supported, and demonstrated from the top.

As a classroom teacher, I was terrible at connecting with my colleagues. I was really good at 'collaborating' with the other Health teachers when I needed something from them, but I was not good at sharing

CHOOSE TO BE YOU

my successes or ideas with them. This stems back to my need to gain approval from others, so in my mind, if I did everything on my own, I would be able to hide my failures or take all the credit for any success I achieved. This carried over into my coaching. When I became a head coach, I tried to do it all on my own. If any of my assistant coaches are reading this, I am sure that they are all laughing out loud as I say this, but I was absolutely terrible at delegating responsibilities. I felt as though I had to do it all myself. I thought that if I delegated responsibilities to one of my assistant coaches, and if it went well, they would get the credit, and I wouldn't. Or, if it didn't go well, all the blame would go to me because I was the head coach. This was rooted in my lack of self-confidence, and my need to prove to everyone that I could do it all by myself!

Looking back on it now, I kick myself for being so stubborn and selfish as a coach. I have been surrounded by some of the best high school coaches I have ever known, but I didn't unleash them to do their best work. I can only imagine how much more successful our teams would have been had I been willing, and strong enough, to share responsibilities with my assistant coaches. I am slowly getting better at this, and need to be constantly reminded about the power of collaboration.

As an Assistant Principal, my primary area of focus is our school's climate and culture. Pretty cool, right?! I truly believe that I have the absolute best Assistant Principal job in the world! I remember being super excited when I first stepped into the role, only to then be overwhelmed and unsure of where to start just a few days in. You see, although it sounds fun and exciting to be responsible for climate and culture, it can also be extremely intimidating depending on the situation and the current state of both the climate and culture at your school. When I started in my AP role, we were not in a great place.

I did not apply for my current job as Assistant Principal. I was asked to step into the role as an interim AP as our principal had announced his resignation. At the time, we also had an interim Superintendent, who appointed an interim principal for the upcoming school year. The challenge for our staff and students was that this was the fourth principal at our high school in the past five years. Before that, we had transitioned from four small schools into one comprehensive high school. Needless to say, we were lacking any sort of continuity and there was not a lot of trust in the administration, simply because there had been so much turnover and change in such a short amount of time.

As great as it was to be an AP in charge of climate and culture, you can imagine the stress I began to feel as I started to think about the work that we needed to do. Luckily for me, and for our school, the Jostens Renaissance family came into my life that same summer! If you have not connected with Jostens Renaissance, you are missing out! The best way to explain Jostens Renaissance is that it is a family of rockstar educators, who are all passionately on fire for education, and want to share all of their amazing ideas with everyone else! Seriously! It's that simple, and that awesome! For me though, Jostens Renaissance has become so much more than just idea-sharing. Jostens Renaissance has opened my eyes to what education is all about, which is finding the best in each and every individual Staffulty member and student, and then finding ways to celebrate them for being who they are as individuals! More on Jostens Renaissance to come!!

When it comes to building school climate and culture, I could write an entire book on that topic alone. And hey, maybe one day I will! But at the root of it all is relationships! Climate is all about how people feel when they walk in the building. If they sense a climate of belonging and acceptance, they are more likely to positively engage as an active and contributing member of the school. Culture is all about shared beliefs and behaviors amongst a group of people. If people feel connected and united in thought and action with others, they are more likely to positively engage in the school community.

To build both a positive school climate and culture, you must start with building relationships!

For some educators this is simple, basic, and common sense. If you are an educator, why did you choose education as your career? Was it solely your love for academics? I'm willing to bet you also wanted to connect with and support student learning and growth. They wanted to connect with and support students! Unfortunately, we as educators sometimes forget that. We get bogged down with the daily grind and bombarded with legislative details. It can get in the way of us doing our best work with students. As the years go by, educators can lose their passion and spark for education. I have seen way too many educators who simply come to work, punch the time clock, and exit the building at the end of the day without intentionally engaging in positive relationships with students or colleagues. Or worse, school leaders who have forgotten that investing deeply in relationships should be a priority in their buildings!

Nothing is more important to the success of our schools than RELATIONSHIPS! If you want to have the best and most successful school, invest fully in RELATIONSHIPS above everything else!

No initiative, no technology, and no mark on a state report card can replace the role of relationships in educating our students!

We know how important relationships are. We know how important school climate and culture are. The question remains, how do we make it a priority?

PEOPLE NEED TANGIBLE REMINDERS

We created a visual reminder to staff. A sign was painted in our main hallway. The words "I'll Do Whatever It Takes" were written across the wall and all Staffulty members signed their name, showing everyone that enters our building that we as educators are dedicated to doing *Whatever It Takes* to help our students be successful. Each fall, we have our newly hired staff members add their names to the wall. The first year we did it was a very powerful moment where our returning staff, who had already signed the wall the

year before, lined the hallway and sang our Alma Mater as the new staff walked through the hall on their way to add their signatures. It was an incredibly meaningful way to initiate and welcome our new staffulty!

The second year, we made silicone wristbands with the same statement, so that not only are people reminded of their commitment every time they walk through the hall, but they could also wear it on their wrist each day as a reminder.

FIRST IMPRESSIONS

Last year, during in-service, just before we released teachers after our final professional development session, I got on the microphone and instructed teachers to NOT give out their syllabus on the first day of school. I explained that students are never more excited about school than on the first day, so we needed to make sure to harness that natural energy and use it to engage them right from the beginning! I told teachers that the only thing we needed them to do with students on Day 1 was to love them and let them know that while they are at school this year, that they will be surrounded by educators who are more concerned with who they are as individuals than who they are as students on paper and in the grade book.

INVESTING IN RELATIONSHIPS

That investment is all about committing to the call of *Choose To Be You*. If my students know that the most important thing to me is that they feel loved and supported to be their best selves, to be who they are, then we can tackle and conquer whatever academic or personal challenges we face. If students know that you've got their back, and if we allow them to fully be who they are, they will run through walls for us! On the flip side, if students only feel pressure from us to be successful academically, and that they have to fit into a specific mold in order for us to approve of them, we limit their ability to be creative and innovative. I am learning more and more that when we can unleash students and be facilitators of their education, rather than the directors of it, amazing things will happen! As educators, our job is to facilitate a rigorous and relevant learning experience for students, and support them in chasing their dreams while constantly reinforcing the message of *Choose To Be You!*

GUT CHECK

As an **individual**, think of a time when you felt immediately welcomed into a new group of people.

THE VALUE OF A CRUSHED PENNY

What was it about how others treated you that made you feel like you belonged?

As a **learner**, think about your favorite educator. Now, write down what it is about that educator that drew you to them. My guess is that the majority of what you write down has everything to do with who they are or how they encouraged you to be who you are, and has nothing to do with their pedagogical approach to instruction.

As an **educator**, what can you do in your school to put the emphasis back on relationships? Depending on the role you are in, what can you do on a daily basis to make sure that students know you love them and that you want to support them in being who they are?

FOUR

DOWNTOWN BROWN

The high school I attended was on the same campus as a small college, and we shared athletic facilities. The college had priority over the soccer field for practices, so we practiced off campus at a nearby park. After school, we would all cram into cars and drive about half a mile down the hill. The older players thought it was funny to sometimes leave us underclassmen behind and make us run to the park. This wasn't a huge deal for most because it was so close, but at 5'2" tall and nearly 180 pounds, any extra running was difficult, especially when I had to carry both my backpack and athletic bag with me. I learned to deal with it and didn't let it bother me too much.

The real issues surfaced when we finally made it to the park. Our coach didn't work at the high school and was often arriving to practice right at the start, as such we were often left unsupervised. When the younger players finally made it to the field, the upperclassmen were there waiting and had been scheming as to how they were going to 'initiate' us into the team. As speed wasn't my strength, it was not easy for me to escape when they would chase me. It quickly became a fun game for the upperclassmen to chase me down and give me a wedgie - sometimes to the point of dragging me across the grass until my underwear literally ripped off. I actually learned that it was better if I cut holes in the base of the waistband so that they would rip and come off more easily when they began pulling on them. This was a regular occurrence.

We did a lot of running at soccer practice. We had one drill that our coach called the 'Grand Tour'. It was a lap around the entire park. It was probably a little over a mile. In an attempt at building teamwork, we were made to run it together as a pack. No matter how hard I tried, I could not keep up with the rest of the team. I was so slow that they often had to loop back to me, which frustrated my teammates as it caused more running for them. I couldn't help but recognize that because of my weight, I was different from everyone else. What made it worse was that on days when I wasn't wearing underwear or spandex sliders, I developed a super bad rash on the inside of my thighs. It got so bad that I would bleed. Not only was I ashamed of not being able to keep up with the rest of the team, but I was also in unbelievable physical pain. What was I supposed to do? The only way to deal with it would be to stand up for myself, or to reach out for help from my coach or another adult and there was no way I was going to do that. That would be a sure-fire way for me to not be accepted at all with the other players, and I didn't want to seem weak. I wanted to fit in. So, instead of courageously standing up for myself, I allowed them to treat me this way in order to be accepted, even if it meant daily physical and emotional pain.

GUT CHECK

As an **individual**, has there ever been a time where you wanted to stand up and advocate for yourself, but didn't feel like you could? What made you feel like you were not able to?

As a **learner**, who is an educator that you can go to when you have an issue? Identify the adult in your building that you trust and respect, and who you know would be there to listen and support you if you needed someone to talk to about a problem you might be facing.

As an **educator**, what can you do to be aware of situations where students might be getting bullied, or having a difficult time fitting in? What can you do to recognize when this is happening, and then be prepared to step in and intervene?

The soccer season ended and the basketball season began. Our school was a perennial powerhouse in basketball. We always made it to the state championship tournament and even took 2nd place three years in a row. It was widely accepted that the basketball players were the most popular kids in school. Though I had quit playing basketball in middle school, I decided that if I wanted to fit in, I'd better join the team.

My lack of athleticism and speed were even more evident and exposed on the basketball court than on the soccer field. What I did have going for me however was the fact that I could shoot the ball. In fact, this was the first time in my life that I gained confidence in basketball, because my junior varsity coach, Coach Cross, nicknamed me "Downtown Brown". I loved it! He never once made me feel ashamed. He did the exact opposite. He focused on what I could do, and built me up with encouragement and motivation! To this day, I keep in contact with Coach Cross and he has supported me in my own basketball coaching journey. He is one of the biggest sources of inspiration and most positive people that I have ever had in my life, and I am forever thankful to him for that.

As educators, this is such an important and powerful lesson for us. So often, students are taught to focus on what they can't do, or what their flaws are. As the adults and people who students look up to for guidance, we are blessed with the opportunity to turn the tables and build them up with confidence by loving them for who they are, and by teaching them to focus their energy on what they can do as opposed to always pointing out to them what they can't do. Every student has unique skills, talents, gifts, and abilities. We must make every *effort* to find what makes a single student special, and do whatever we can to bring positive attention to that student to help build up their confidence in who they are, while also showing others what makes that student unique and beautiful. I'll never forget the impact that Coach Cross made on me by simply calling me "Downtown Brown" and never shaming me for what I couldn't do, but always praising me for what I could do.

Think back to your experience in school. When your teachers only focused on things you struggled with, how did it make you feel? I'm guessing not great. We have to give those we serve constructive feedback and help them work through specific areas of growth. We must be intentional about making sure that they feel valued and understand that we see the positive things they can do and have accomplished. We also need to help them learn and grow in areas where they are not as strong and use mistakes as teachable moments.

When we are constantly told that we are not good enough, or when only our flaws and inabilities seem to be noticed by others, it creates a negative self-view. Unfortunately, our overwhelming access to media finds today's students creating a negative self-view earlier in their lives than ever before. When all we see through social media are the amazing things that other people have accomplished and what others can do, we tend to think that we are not as good and that we are inadequate compared to others.

This is a common struggle in educators as well. As we see others posting about their accomplishments as professionals, publishing books, delivering keynote addresses, we can quickly begin to think that we are falling behind and that they are superior. We are quick to compare. Instead of being proud of them and excited for their accomplishments, we can become jealous and disappointed in ourselves. When we intentionally celebrate students' uniquenesses and abilities, we can help them work through the comparison struggle. After all, as Roosevelt said, comparison is the thief of joy.

I love how my good friend Dr. Phillip Campbell puts it. He says that we need to make sure that all students feel seen, heard, and loved. As educators, Dr. Campbell challenges us to be able to say,

"I see you, I hear you, and I love you"

to all students we interact with. This was a shift to how I originally viewed my role as an educator. As a young teacher, I was conflicted because I wanted to be the cool teacher, but I also thought that I needed to be the rule enforcer and had to keep a thick and strong barrier between myself and students so that they always knew who was boss. Thanks to mentors like Dr. Campbell, I quickly learned that my greatest responsibility as a classroom teacher, coach, and now as an administrator, is to love my students unconditionally. Before we can expect them to be successful academically, they need to know that we will support them and that we have their back no matter what life throws at them. Some of our students come from such broken homes and have life experiences we can't even begin to imagine. Being academically successful at school may be the last thing on their minds. If we as educators meet and support our students where they are, and as who they are, there is a greater chance of them feeling valued and they are more likely to engage positively in their education. Sometimes all it takes is a simple nickname like "Downtown Brown" to completely change the trajectory of a student's life.

GUT CHECK

As an **individual**, when you are working and interacting with others, do you first recognize and find their abilities and strengths, or are you quicker to find their weaknesses and their inabilities? How can you make sure to always find the good in people first, and then make sure to point out what you see so that they are encouraged and built up positively?

As a **learner**, who is that educator that made you feel special and recognized your abilities instead of just your inabilities? I challenge you to reach out to that educator and let them know the impact they had on your life.

As an **educator**, when was the last time you told your students "I Love You." If you have never said this to students, why not?

I can't begin to imagine where I would be in life if it wasn't for Coach Cross. To be honest, my basketball career should probably have ended after my sophomore year of high school. Believing there was no way I would make varsity as a junior, I decided to quit. It seemed easier for me to self-select out of the program, rather than face the disappointment of sitting on the bench all year. Coach Cross wouldn't let me quit that easily though. His encouragement and our connection made me change my mind. As a result, my junior year was one of the best years of basketball I'd ever had. I was a captain on the JV team and loved playing for Coach Cross, embracing the role of 'Downtown Brown' and working to become the best three-point shooter possible.

As a junior, I was often called up to sit on the bench during varsity games. As we moved into the postseason, I began practicing with the varsity team full time. The reality was that I couldn't keep up at the varsity level. I struggled with the idea that as a senior, at this pace, I would spend all season sitting on the bench. I knew I couldn't quit again, so I decided that I was going to be committed to losing weight and getting myself in shape so that I could compete at the varsity level.

I started running.

.

FIVE

RUNNING FOR MY LIFE

One of my favorite memories as a young kid was going on "Run Rides" with my dad. My dad was always super active and he ran a lot. He participated in team distance relays and marathons. When we were kids, we would join him on his runs by riding our bikes alongside him. I loved this time with my dad! It really wasn't physical exercise for me, but more of an opportunity to spend time with him. My dad always did a great job of including us kids in his life. He always let us participate with him in whatever activities he was doing, whether it be through "Run Rides," helping him with yard work, or letting us go to the office with him and hang out while he worked. I learned a lot about parenting and teaching from my dad through these moments. He taught me about the importance of having my kids, both my children and my students, see me as who I truly and authentically am by inviting them into my life to walk alongside me in whatever I am doing. I think for a lot of parents and educators, we feel like we must compartmentalize our lives and keep personal, professional, and family all separate. I completely disagree with that approach!

We must always be exactly who we are, in all areas of our lives!

As individuals, we must be committed to living life authentically, while fully engaging with whoever is around us!

As I got older, my exercise came through my participation in sports, but I was never committed to any type of personal fitness. I'll never forget my first run after my junior year of high school as I started working towards getting in shape for my senior year. It was miserable! We lived out in the country and our house was up on a small hill. When you got to the main road at the bottom of our hill, it was about half a mile down to the stop sign that connected with the main road. I walked down the hill and started jogging towards the stop sign. I was 5'4" tall, and 205 pounds by this point. I didn't even make it halfway to the stop sign. I had to start walking. I finished the one mile out and back route, switching between jogging and walking, in just less than fifteen minutes. I was exhausted and couldn't imagine why anyone would do this for fun on a regular basis! My mom has always said that I was one stubborn kid and I was not about to let one miserable run ruin my goal and desire to lose weight and get in shape. I kept running.

As I ran more and more, I also started to eat healthier. I cut out sugar. I noticed that I started feeling more energetic, and was actually feeling like I was losing weight. I made sure to check the scale every single morning and night. Though, if I was up in weight at the end of the day, I considered myself a failure. As the pounds started falling off, I became more and more excited about losing weight and started to enjoy exercise and the healthier eating habits. Looking back on it now, I realized that I was becoming addicted to exercise and losing weight. This was the opening of the door into a long, dark, painful next chapter of my life. Anorexia.

I began waking up early to run before school and then again in the evenings. Once summer came, I exercised before work, after work, and on my days off. I worked maintenance out at a youth camp, so not only was I exercising by running once or twice a day, I was also getting a physical workout all day long through manual labor. We were so busy with full camps seven days a week. I often missed meals because the only time I could get into the cabins for maintenance was when our campers were in the dining hall. At least that was the excuse I used. Early on, I found ways to hide my anorexia, because I didn't want others noticing or asking why I wasn't eating. I was losing weight at an unhealthy rate. From the end of March to the middle of August, I lost over 50lbs! I dropped from 205lbs down to 150lbs by the time soccer workouts began for my senior season. I was suddenly not only keeping up during workouts, but I was often at the front of the pack! Because I had been running so much, my cardio was the best it had ever been, and I had more stamina than most of my teammates. I felt great!

After moving back home at the end of summer, I continued to find ways to miss meals. There were days that I would not eat even one full meal. I was on my own for breakfast, and would often eat just a granola bar. For lunch, I would maybe eat a piece of fruit. The most difficult meal to skip was dinner, because my mom would have a hot, home-cooked meal ready for me when I got home from practice. I eventually found ways to avoid dinner too. I lived about 30 minutes away from my high school and was responsible for driving myself to and from school. I got up early and left the house to beat rush hour traffic, and then each afternoon, I had soccer or basketball practice, so I would often not get home until after 7pm. Sometimes, I would hang out with my friends after practice and would call to tell my parents that I was eating dinner with them, so there was no need for my mom to keep dinner ready for me at home. I quickly learned that if I did this, I could get out of having to eat an entire meal, and could instead just lightly snack and graze. In fact, I became really good at grazing. I taught myself that if I didn't eat an entire cookie, or just ate a few bites of a sandwich, that it wouldn't impact my weight gain. This was a way for me to not only trick others, but I started to trick myself. I convinced myself that if I nibbled on something, then I wasn't fully denying myself food, but I also wasn't putting unwanted extra calories into my body. I became a permanent snacker, rarely eating a full meal. If I did have to eat an entire meal because I was at an event or sitting down with my family for a meal, I was really good about only taking small portions. And then after eating that meal, I knew that I could make up for indulging in a full meal by not eating as much over the next day or so.

Anorexia is about so much more than just not eating food. It is a disorder where your brain gets wired in a way that you are constantly obsessed and thinking about food and eating. Everything I did revolved around my next meal. All of my actions were strategically planned out to make sure that I had control over my food and that people would not notice my food avoidance. It had complete control over every single aspect and area of my life and breeds indescribable pressure that often turns into shame and self-loathing.

As fall began to wind down and my senior basketball season got closer, I noticed that I had a lot of pain in my ankle. I didn't let the pain stop me from competing in soccer, or from going on my regular daily runs. I knew I had to be in the best possible shape for basketball season. It's what I had spent the past several months working so hard for. In my second to last soccer game, I remember getting taken down by a slide tackle and was in excruciating pain. I came out of the game and could not go back in. When I woke up the next morning, I nearly collapsed as I stepped out of bed and tried to walk. I experienced more pain than the day before. I knew something wasn't right. The doctors discovered two bone spurs that were irritating the ligaments in the ankle. I was going to need surgery. I was devastated. I would miss the first half of the basketball season. I felt like everything I had worked so hard for was suddenly gone.

My surgery was scheduled during the first week of basketball practices. I remember going to the first two practices, sitting on the sidelines and watching my teammates compete. I was absolutely defeated. I tried to have an upbeat attitude, but it was hard.

The surgery was successful. I went back to school and returned to practice as soon as I was able to. I sat there, watching and waiting in my boot for the moment that I could return to the court. I remember the day I finally got to put my uniform on. I felt like my time had come! I was ready to take the floor and would finally be the basketball star that I had always dreamed of being! I went through warmups and got myself locked in the zone mentally. I was ready! The first quarter ended, and I was still on the bench. We headed into the locker room for halftime and I still had my warmup on. By the end of the third quarter, I started to realize that I was not going to be in the official rotation. At the end of the game, I gave myself a pep talk and decided that instead of sulking and complaining, I was going to use this as motivation to work that much harder.

I worked as hard as I could, on and off the court. I was running in the morning, working out during PE class, gave my all in practice, and would finish the day with another run. I continued with my eating habits of skipping meals and snacking randomly throughout the day, and the weight continued to fall off. By this point, I was down to about 135lbs, which meant that in less than 10 months, I had lost 70 pounds. Despite all of my hard work, I still wasn't seeing any playing time during games.

Reflecting back, I completely understand why my head coach kept me out of the rotation. The only thing I was able to do well was shoot. Even though I had gotten myself in shape and was able to keep up with the pace of the game, I had not spent any time working on my ball-handling skills. I could not handle the ball at varsity level. I was an offensive liability for my team. At the time, however I didn't understand. I was frustrated and upset. I felt like I had worked so hard, for nothing. The season ended and I only ever saw court time at the end of games if we were up by a lot. I was often embarrassed and can even remember telling my coach that I didn't want to go in with less than 2 minutes left when we were up by more than 20 points. It was humiliating to be receiving pity minutes as a senior.

It was nearly impossible to focus on anything besides the fact that I was not getting the playing time I wanted. Instead of focusing my energy on what I could control, I was focusing on what I couldn't. This is one thing that I have really tried to champion and teach my players as a basketball coach. In life, we only get to control three things: *Our Attitude, Our Effort,* and *How We Treat Others.* We can often focus on things outside of our control. When we do this, we are often disappointed, unsatisfied, and become bitter towards our situation, and towards others.

As individuals, we must never let the things outside of our control dictate our next move. We can't control the weather, traffic or grocery store lineups. Students don't always have control of their schedules, the cafeteria menu and the behavior of their peers. As educators, we may not be in control of our class lists, new initiatives from administration and decisions our colleagues make.

There will always be things that are outside of our control. When life happens, we have to choose where and how we focus our energy. We have to intentionally commit to putting all of our *effort* into things that we have the ability to control. When we do this, and we keep a positive-centered attitude, we have a much greater opportunity to be successful. Additionally, when we have a positive *attitude* and we are giving intentional and positive *effort* towards things that improve our situation as an individual in healthy ways, it is much more natural to be positive, kind, and loving towards others.

Embracing the call to Choose To Be You means learning to control the controllables of our attitude, effort, and how we treat others.

A perfect example of this idea in action is the current situation happening in our lives, our schools, and around the world. As I am writing this book, we are in the middle of the COVID-19 global pandemic. You will recall the chaos and unknowns that we all experienced as the situation unfolded. You have surely heard about the major changes that the world went through during the COVID-19 Pandemic. As an individual and a school leader who is currently in the midst of this unprecedented time, it is surreal to be living through this experience. I never imagined that we would ever be in a position to close the doors of our schools in the middle of a school year. For many educators, it has meant not seeing students and colleagues, face-to-face, for maybe five or six months. This is not how we "do" school! What about our seniors who are planning to graduate this year and go to college in the fall? Our underclassmen who are supposed to move to the next grade level are missing out on quality, standards-based instruction that they need as a prerequisite for their next class. What about our students from low-income families who qualify for free or reduced lunch and rely on at least two meals each day from school? I keep thinking that there is no way this could all be real and actually happening...but it is. And it's all out of my control.

I am so incredibly inspired and encouraged by so many school leaders around the country who are focusing their *attitude* and *effort* on things that they have the ability to control and have an impact on. As I scroll through social media, my feed is flooded with examples of people who are doing the absolute best they can on behalf of others! Rather than complaining and blaming the current situation for how it is impacting our schools, we are collaborating more powerfully than ever before. We are increasing our creativity for how we 'do' school every single day!

Almost all schools immediately set up food distribution centers or action plans to make sure that all students still had access to daily meals. Educators are engaging in some of the most meaningful and productive collaboration, via video calls and conferences, that I have ever witnessed! Schools and communities across the nation are beautifully modeling what it means to *Choose To Be You* by focusing every ounce of *effort* on taking care of each other, and doing it with a positive *attitude*!

Probably the most encouraging thing I've witnessed and experienced through this experience is how it has brought people together and strengthened bonds and relationships. Although we are actively practicing social distancing and limiting the amount of in-person contact we have, there is more social connection right now than almost ever before. I'd almost like to think of it in terms of physical distancing because socially, we are stronger than ever! Educators are connecting daily with others all around the world and are sharing ideas, spreading encouragement, and simply taking the time to check-in with one another. When you *Choose To Be You* it requires you to fully invest in your community, and be an active participant in spreading positivity and contributing towards the greater good for others. Once you have found solace and confidence in embracing who you are, you then have a responsibility to be an example of *Choose To Be You* to others, and support others in embracing who they are.

By extending grace, understanding, and support to others, you allow others to find the same freedom and joy you have found in the journey of Choose To Be You.

You cannot find who you are on your own. Once you have found who you are, make the effort to support and encourage others to find who they are.

Whenever there is a high level of need, people tend to rise to the occasion and we often see the best versions of people when there is an emergency. When there is a community need people tend to band together and collaborate better than ever to make sure the needs of the greater community are met. But why? Why does it have to take a natural disaster, a student suicide, the death of an educator, or some other catastrophic event for people to be their best selves? My hope through the COVID-19 experience is that we realize how much we can accomplish when we work together and that we continue to embrace creativity in solving problems.

As the world continues to evolve and change, we must be looking for ways and opportunities to adjust our approach to how we 'do' education. Hopefully, by being forced to do school differently than ever before, we look at ways to make lasting and permanent changes. This has created an opportunity for us to pivot in our approach to education. Our students deserve it, and our educators are ready to make it happen! As educational leaders, we need to be bold enough to support the changes. We need to take a long, hard look at what our student's greatest areas of need are and make necessary changes in response.

It would be a shame, if after this, schools go back to existing as they were before this pandemic. We cannot waste the strong bonds and relationships that are being formed through this time of need. We cannot waste the innovative ways that educators are responding to this sudden change in education. School is so much more than just a place where students come to learn reading, writing, and math. For so many of our students, school is their safe place. School is where they come to get hot meals. School is where they receive the mental health supports they would not otherwise have access to. School is where students come to feel loved by caring educators, each and every day. School is where students learn how to *Choose To Be You!*

We have an opportunity to give our students a better, more dynamic, and more empowering education than anyone else before now has ever had the opportunity to experience! We need to treat each day as an emergency situation! Each day, we have students who walk into our classrooms, expecting and needing us to give our best as educators. We don't know what stress or challenges an individual student might be walking into our classrooms with. What may seem like a 'normal' day to us could be the most important day of that student's life! Each day is an opportunity to love students and to encourage and empower them to embrace the *Choose To Be You* mentality. As educators, we need to declare a 'State of Emergency' each and every day, because every day we have with students is critical! We cannot afford to waste or miss a single moment! Every day, students are pressured into being someone and something besides their true selves, and that's not acceptable. Educators have the responsibility to fight for each individual student who is in our care. We have a duty to focus on what is in our control: Our *Attitude*, Our *Effort*, and *How We Treat Students*. We need to advocate for their rights and experiences. Educators everywhere must commit to ensuring that all students have the opportunity, safety, and understanding of what it takes to *Choose To Be You*.

Life is best when it is shared and experienced with others.

We must always look for opportunities to positively connect with others, by being our authentic self. When we can live life with a positive *attitude*, by giving our best *effort* regardless of the uncontrollable, and we *Treat Others* with love, grace, and acceptance, then we have truly found what it means to *Choose To Be You*.

GUT CHECK
As an **individual**, what are things in your daily life that are outside of your control, but that often

impact your attitude? What can you do to make sure that you keep your focus completely on only the things that are within your control?

As a **learner**, what keeps you from giving your best *effort* in school? What regular reminders do you need to help make sure that you are always giving your absolute best *effort*, regardless of things that happen, which are outside of your control?

As an **educator**, what can you do to foster a classroom and school environment that encourages learners to focus only on what they can control: Attitude, Effort, and How We Treat Others?

CHAPTER

GUT CHECK

As my senior basketball season ended, I was not quite sure what was supposed to happen next. I did not play a spring sport, so I suddenly had a lot of free time. I was still struggling with the feeling of failure. I hadn't reached my goal of becoming a contributing player on my varsity basketball team. I felt that I still needed to prove myself.

I have always been goal-oriented, in healthy and unhealthy ways. I have always needed something to work towards, to feel and show that I accomplished something. This was part of my own struggle with showing others how good I was and needing their approval, rather than just being who I truly was. I began to turn my full attention to running. By committing to running a marathon, I would have an excuse for all of the excessive running and dieting I was continuing to participate in. My dad committed to running the Portland marathon with me later that year. With a goal in front of me centered around running, my workouts and minimal eating went to a whole new extreme. I continued to lose weight, getting as low at 130lbs at one point. Over the course of one year, I'd lost 75lbs and measured only 5'5" tall.

I was planning to attend Pepperdine University in Malibu, California on a full-ride scholarship. My dad and all three uncles had attended Pepperdine, so I was following in their footsteps and had never really even considered any other colleges. Pepperdine is a prestigious university, so it gave me a sense of status to be able to tell people that's where I was planning to go. However, little did I know that my plans were about to drastically change.

The summer after high school graduation found me working back at the youth camp with a long time friend. Sarah and I had a connection, and before the summer was over, we started dating. The only problem with our quickly established summer romance was that it would suddenly become a long-distance relationship as she headed off to Oklahoma and I to California for school. In my mind there was really only one solution. I wasn't going to let her go off to Oklahoma by herself. The only option was for me to go with her. She tried to talk me out of it. On paper and in almost any rational person's brain, this was not a wise decision. I'd be giving up a full ride scholarship and there were no guarantees that I would even be accepted. But for me, this was the first time that I felt like I was making my own decisions. There was an unfamiliar level of confidence that this was the right choice. It was the first time in my life that I was making a decision based on who I was and what I wanted for me, rather than making a decision because I was chasing an image and persona of who I wanted others to believe I was.

I quickly jumped online to complete the OC application and sent an email to the financial aid department to explain that I was applying and was hoping to put together a financial aid package. But that was only the small hurdle. The bigger hurdle was going to be a conversation with my parents. I am not sure if I have ever been more scared or nervous in my life! I knew that this is what I wanted to do, but I also felt like I was going to be letting my parents down by telling them that I was switching schools.

Let it be known that I in no way endorse high school seniors choosing which college to attend based on their current relationship status, especially when they have only been dating for three weeks, like Sarah and I. But my decision to switch from Pepperdine was not about Sarah. It was about me finally making a decision for myself, based on what I wanted, and not at all because of what I thought others wanted me to do. I was making this decision with boldness and confidence, which is something I had never done before. My parents were surprisingly supportive. Not to say that they were not shocked and worried, but after a few conversations, they understood that this was what I wanted.

I believe there are some major lessons in this story for all of us as we seek to discover what *Choose To Be You* is all about. First, when there is a tough decision to be made, going with your gut is almost always the way to go. When we are faced with a difficult decision, it is important to slow down, consider all of the factors that are playing into the decision, and make sure we do a *Gut Check*. In order to confidently and boldly make a difficult decision, especially when the outcome of the decision will impact not only us but others as well, we had better be a believer in the decisions we are making. Regardless of the outcome, whether the decision leads to a positive or negative experience, we must have full confidence that we are making the absolute best decision possible, for all of the right reasons.

I use the term *Gut Check* because for too long, I constantly did gut checks on myself, but through the lens of how other people viewed me, both literally and figuratively. I chose to change my body because of the way my physical gut looked. I made decisions based on what I thought others wanted and expected from me all the time. When I was faced with the decision of choosing whether or not to switch schools, it was the first time that my *Gut Check* was centered on what I believed was best for me, and what I wanted for my life. It was the first time that I was more focused on who I was in that moment rather than who I was trying to be for others.

When we fully embrace the mentality of *Choose To Be You*, we are forced to engage in some difficult conversations. Part of living life as your authentic self means learning how to advocate for yourself. I'll never forget how nervous I was before telling my parents I wanted to go to Oklahoma with Sarah. I didn't know what to say, so I just blurted it out. There was a long silence. I had definitely caught both of my parents off guard. My mom put her book down and my dad said, "Mark, regardless of your decision or what happens, I hope you know that I'll always love you." Wow! Talk about being able to breathe a sigh of relief! Not that I expected my parents wouldn't love me, but to hear those words and for that to be my dad's immediate response was everything I needed.

Don't get me wrong. It wasn't as easy as that. An intense and heated conversation followed.
All sorts of questions and concerns were brought up.

Luckily, because I had done a *Gut Check* and was confident that this is what I wanted, I had thought through almost all of their questions and concerns ahead of time and had responses ready. After a follow-up conversation the next morning, they told me they were ready to support whatever decision I made, and would be ready to help me navigate whatever hurdles we would have to conquer in order to make it happen.

What I've noticed in my administrative career is that many people often enter into difficult conversations in one of two ways:

- Bold and arrogant, with every intention of winning and dominating the conversation with no respect or regard for what the other person has to say.
- Timid and unable to articulate what they believe is right, or what their gut is telling them. These people are more concerned with keeping peace and avoiding conflict. As a result, they don't advocate for themselves. They allow others to take advantage of them. These are not reciprocal conversations, they are one sided.

Understanding what it means to *Choose To Be You* in difficult conversations requires an intentional *effort* to pause, take a *Gut Check*, build up the confidence and courage to be honest, and then enter into the conversation with the ability to listen and show empathy to the other person, while still articulating one's full truth.

This is still something I struggle with today. People pleasers and those who struggle with self-confidence and self-worth will often let people take advantage of them to avoid conflict. Though these conversations may be uncomfortable, they become much more productive when we enter into them after having done a *Gut Check,* when we intentionally listen for understanding, and when we are confident in what we believe is right and best.

When this happens, people are often calmer and the conversation is reciprocal and respectful. We may realize that our ideas or positions were wrong and adjust our opinions as we become aware of the other person's view. This allows us to walk away from the conversation, regardless of the outcome, with the peace of mind knowing we were true to who we are, and that we showed respect to the other person through the interaction. We control what we can control...ourselves, our reaction, our choices.

GUT CHECK
As an **individual**, how do you deal with difficult conversations? Are you more aggressive or passive?

How can you make sure that you perform a true *Gut Check* before heading into a difficult conversation?

As a **learner**, are you good at listening to others? What do you need to do in order to make sure that you always listen to understand someone's point of view who is on the opposite side of a conversation from you?

As an **educator**, how do you support and encourage students to advocate for themselves? Do you model positive advocacy for your students, which includes showing grace and empathy to others?

CHAPTER
SEVEN

STOPPED IN MY TRACKS

Sarah and I headed off to Oklahoma to begin our college careers. As we settled into our first semester, I was busy training and preparing for my marathon. I ran more and ate less than I ever had before. I remember my first-ever 20-mile training run. I planned it for a Saturday morning. The Friday evening before the run, I drove the route so I could plant water bottles on the side of the road along the way. I left campus, turned left onto Bryant Avenue, and drove straight for 10 miles. For any of you who have ever done any distance running, you realize how ridiculous that plan was. Never, never, never plan a completely straight out and back route for a long-distance training run, especially one that you are doing all by yourself! I also did not run with music, so it was just going to be me, by myself, 10 miles out, and 10 miles back.

It was mid-September. The weather was still hot and humid. I had planned to wake up early and start at 6:00am to beat the heat. I woke up, ate a granola bar, drank a glass of water, and started off on my run! As I should have expected, it was miserable! It was a fairly flat route, but it was straight, and I was all alone. From a running and training standpoint, I ran a little faster than my target pace, so I was happy with that. I made it back to campus in time to get breakfast with friends. Having just finished a 20-mile run, I should have eaten for two, if not more. Not wanting to waste a huge calorie-burning workout, I allowed myself Gatorade, a spoonful of peanut butter, and a bowl of cereal. I remember feeling weak, light-headed, and dizzy, but refused to eat anymore. I slept most of the rest of the day.

The weekend of the marathon arrived. I flew home on a Friday. I was so excited! On the morning of the race it was cool and damp. My mom had bought us all sweatshirts to wear at the start of the race that we could then take off and throw to the side of the route once it warmed up. Volunteers would pick up the sweatshirts, wash them, and donate them to homeless shelters. I remember wearing my sweatshirt all the way to mile 8. Even though most people took them off after only the first few miles, I figured the longer I wore it, the more I would sweat, and the more calories I would burn. I bypassed several water and refueling

STOPPED IN MY TRACKS

stations because I was more focused on finishing the race as fast as possible, to prove to everyone how well I had trained and prepared. I ran a great race. I was under my target time and won my age division. I felt great about what I had accomplished!

As I walked around after the race, there were tables filled with every type of food you could imagine! There were hamburgers, pizza, fruit, smoothies, pop, ice cream, you name it and it was there! I remember allowing myself to grab one serving of ice cream to celebrate, but that was it. Even after having just ran 26.2 miles, I refused to eat because I feared weight gain. This is how sick I was in my battle against anorexia. For those who have never experienced any type of mental illness, it is difficult to understand how powerful and controlling the disease can be. Anorexia controlled me then and still has power over me at times that can be difficult to overcome.

Halfway through our second semester our university announced that they were forming a group to participate in the Oklahoma City Memorial Marathon. There was a 5k, half marathon, full marathon, and a team relay marathon option. Several people were signing up, and there was no way I was going to miss out on this opportunity. I knew that not very many people were going to sign up for the individual full marathon, so I saw it as a way to showcase myself as a marathon runner in front of my peers. I was in great shape and my pace was getting faster. I had a personal goal of qualifying for the Boston Marathon with my next marathon, so I was really pushing myself and training harder than before.

The race was scheduled for the Sunday after finals week. As the race started, I took off at an even faster pace than I had trained for. I was feeling great. The adrenaline gave me way more energy and excitement than I had anticipated having. I was running strong and ahead of my target pace to qualify for Boston. As I hit mile 16, my knee started hurting. I did my best to ignore it and kept my pace. By mile 19, I had slowed down significantly and was beginning to adjust my gate to favor my hurting knee. I continued pushing myself, but by the time I hit mile 22, I could no longer run and had to give in to walking. I was devastated and embarrassed. I got myself to the finish line and several people from my university were there to congratulate me, but I was in no mood to celebrate. I was so disappointed. All I wanted to do was get to the airport and go home.

I discovered that I had developed a severe case of runner's knee. I had damaged much of the cartilage in my knee due to extreme overuse. During my training, there was one point where I went nearly 60 days without a single day of rest. I felt that if I took a day

STOPPED IN MY TRACKS

off, I would fall behind in my training, and that I would gain weight. For me, running was so much more than just training for marathons. Running was a way to continue to burn calories and keep my weight down. Yet another example of the power and control that anorexia had over me and how it influenced the decisions that I made.

Unfortunately, because of my need to constantly prove myself to others, I often tend to take things to the extreme. I fill my life with too many responsibilities and don't know how or when to say 'no.' I convince myself that the busier I am, the more that people will notice me. I equate my busyness to a position of status. This is something I still struggle with today. In fact, as I write this, I am currently an Assistant Principal, Head Varsity Basketball Coach, completing a speaker preparation program, working on my Ed.D., raising a two- and four-year-old, being a husband, and writing my first book. Just listing it all out like that makes me realize how much stuff I have crammed into my life, all with the hopes of proving myself to those around me.

I am thankful for that knee injury. It forced me to slow down and stop pushing myself so hard physically. While I still struggled with shame in eating and continued to deny myself food, the exercise component of my struggle and how that had compounded my illness minimized for the time being.

As I reflect back on the knee injury, I realize that I have always needed a major event to stop me from overdoing myself and forcing me to slow down. I have never done a good job of intentionally resting and focusing on self-care, because in my mind, if I stop making progress in any of the different areas of my life, I am going to fall behind compared to others. As I chased an identity that I thought other people would approve of, I sacrificed my health - physical, emotional, mental, and social. I have put my achievements, accomplishments, and how I thought other people viewed me ahead of my health and ahead of my relationships.

The current situation in our world is just another example of being forced to slow down. Education as we've known it has been stopped in its tracks. School buildings are closed, international travel is limited, only a few essential businesses remain open and operating as normal, but most everything has shut down. As school leaders, we are busy trying to move our entire academic system to a distance learning model, all from home and via video conferencing. At first, I struggled with the adjustment to this new norm. I was still going into the school building each day. I felt I needed to and that I wasn't being a good administrator if I wasn't there. I have slowly learned to embrace and enjoy our new routine. Though busy while working from home, I am getting to spend a lot more time with my wife and daughters. I am running and exercising (responsibly) more regularly than I have in years and living a much slower pace of life, which is forcing me to realize how busy and consumed in my job I had become.

I had pushed such a fast pace of life for so long, that it just became normal and routine. Having been forced to stop and slow down as a result of school closures made me realize how much my family has had to sacrifice because of my constant need and desire to fill my plate with something else and something more. It would be impossible not to notice the difference when you move from 13 hour days to being home full time. I went from spending 20 minutes with my daughters on some days to suddenly being able to spend almost every waking minute with them! As with my knee injury, I am grateful for this unexpected time at home. It has forced me to slow down in my professional life and allowed me to be completely present in my personal life.

As educators, we can often overcommit and spread ourselves too thin. For those of us who are passionate about our work, we often have a problem saying 'no.' It can sometimes feel that if we're not at every event or on every committee, we are not doing enough. I definitely struggle with connecting how busy I am at work with my status in other people's eyes. I have often felt that the busier and more involved I was at school, the more respect I'd earn. It is important that we find a structure for our time so we can maintain full commitment in each arena of our life.

I recently listened to an education-based podcast where the guest was speaking about managing and juggling the various responsibilities of work and home. She spoke of the work - life balance. She challenged the idea that it's not about balance, but rather prioritizing your presence. There are different seasons of life where more attention and energy is needed in different areas. However, no matter how busy we are at home or at school, we need to be completely present in that arena when I am there.

Wherever I am needs to be my priority at that moment.

Educators tend to prioritize our presence at school. We may even find it difficult to prioritize our presence when we are at home with our families. When we bring work home, we are not prioritizing our presence with our families. On nights when I don't bring a pile of work home, I am often so exhausted that I head straight to the couch. I may not be consumed with work, but I am so physically, mentally, and emotionally drained from the day that I am not able to prioritize my presence with my wife and daughters. What I have realized is that my family has sacrificed so much to support me in my work as both an administrator and a basketball coach, and through that sacrifice, they have suffered from me not making them the priority when I am present with them.

As discussed in previous chapters, if we are going to commit to something, we must give our absolute best *effort*. It is very likely that you are always giving your best *effort* at work, but if we have committed ourselves in too many areas, we tend to sacrifice our *effort* at home with our family. I have soared and thrived in my career, but I have compromised the health of my family in doing so. *Choose To Be You* and giving your best means always giving your best *effort* without having to pick and choose when. This forced time at home has made many of us realize how bad I had been at prioritizing my presence with my family. The challenge for me is going to be once the COVID-19 pandemic is over, what does 'normal' look like? My new 'normal' will need to look different than it did before COVID-19. I will need to analyze all of my commitments and decide what needs to be changed and adjusted so that I can make sure to give my best *effort* and be fully present in each arena of my life, without compromising or sacrificing another area.

My challenge to you as a reader would be to reflect on all of the different commitments you have in your life.

Consider work and personal commitments, and the areas of life where you spend time. Think about which areas are easier and more difficult to prioritize your presence in. Think about whether or not you need to make some changes in your commitments so that you can be sure to always give your best *effort*. This is not easy. It takes a deep level of vulnerability to answer these questions honestly with yourself and make these changes. This is a big step towards living the *Choose To Be You* lifestyle.

GUT CHECK

As an **individual**, have you ever become so obsessed with something that it has controlled your life? If so, what do you need to do in order to slow down and make sure that you are not giving too much *effort* in a specific area, that it is taking away from other areas of your life?

As a **learner**, what can you do to make sure that as you gain more responsibility and get busier, you are able to manage your commitments and not become over-committed and stretched too thin?

As an **educator**, are you committing so much to your work, that you are unable to prioritize your presence at home? Or, are you so over-committed in multiple areas at work, that you feel as though you might not be able to give your best *effort* in each area? What changes might you need to make to be sure that you are able to prioritize your presence and give your best *effort* in each area of both work and personal life?

CHAPTER

EIGHT

CHASING TITLES

I spent the following semester studying abroad in Europe, so my schedule was not very conducive to running and training since we were traveling and backpacking around the continent for three months. I am very thankful for my semester spent in Europe and how it came at just the right time. It provided a distraction for me from the fact that I could no longer run and train as I wanted. It was the perfect opportunity at a time when I needed it most in my life. I often wonder how I would have coped and dealt with not being able to run if I had not been away that semester. I am grateful I never had to face that reality. I'm not sure I would have been prepared to deal with it in a healthy way at that time in my life.

Like all good things, my time in Europe came to an end. Once I was back on campus, I quickly began feeling pressure to do more. I remember feeling inadequate because I was no longer doing anything above and beyond. I was just being a *regular* college student. I could not deal with the 'mediocre' lifestyle I felt like I was living. I began brainstorming and thinking about what I should do. I naturally gravitated towards sports and athletics. I think subconsciously, I still felt that I had something to prove when it came to basketball. I had worked so hard in the sport, but never achieved the success I so desperately wanted. I was smart enough to realize that there was no way I would ever be able to play college basketball, so trying out was out of the question. I figured that there had to be a way to get involved. Lucky for me, I have never been shy about asking for something, so I reached out to the head coach at my university, and asked if there were any opportunities to get involved with the program.

I was a Physical Education major and had thought for a while that coaching was something I wanted to do. I had taken a couple of classes with Coach Hays in the P.E. Department, so I knew I would enjoy working for him if given the opportunity. Thankfully, he was very open to my request to join the program, and he gave me the opportunity to join his staff as a student assistant coach. I could not wait to get started!

Knowing that Coach Hays was already in the Hall of Fame, I was excited to learn from him!

Once I returned to campus in the fall for my junior year, I spent every single second that I was not in class in the gym. I became a coaching junkie and did not want to miss out on any opportunity to learn and be engaged in whatever the coaching staff was doing. Looking back on it, I am humbled by how Coach Hays and the rest of the coaches welcomed me into being a member of the coaching staff. Even though I was still a student, they included me in everything from scheme planning, to recruiting trips, to going to watch the Oklahoma City Thunder practice, and even taking me to the national coaching convention at the Final Four! Coach Hays treated me just like he did any of his other assistants. My title didn't matter. He was happy to let me learn and be involved in everything. I was blessed to see and do way more than I ever thought possible, simply because Coach Hays welcomed me into his coaching staff with open arms.

As educators and educational leaders, this is an important lesson for us as we work with students and staffulty. As leaders, we have an incredible opportunity to empower and include others in our work. Too often, we develop and create unofficial hierarchy systems in education. We let titles and personal agendas get in the way of allowing people to be included, or to be given freedom to do their best work. This is something I have struggled with. I was of the mindset that if I was the one doing all of the work, I would get the credit for it. This is dangerous and unhealthy. When we learn to *Choose To Be You,* we learn to be confident in who we are, and that it is not about getting the credit, but about accomplishing something great for the betterment of others and our organization. As long as good things are happening in our schools, does it really matter who gets the credit? As a young leader, this is something I continue to work on. I am learning that when I include and empower others, amazing things happen! I am limited in what I can do and accomplish on my own. I am learning to find joy in others' success.

The best leaders find the greatest joy in the accomplishments of others.

They go out of their way to celebrate the accomplishments of those that they lead.

GUT CHECK

As an **individual**, have you ever been welcomed into a group that you wanted to belong to? How did it make you feel when you felt accepted, and you didn't even have to do anything specific to prove yourself or your worth?

As a **learner**, which educators have empowered you in your learning? I encourage you to reach out to those educators who have played a major role in your development through supporting and empowering you and let them know how much you appreciate them.

As an **educator**, do you invite others to be active participants in your work and empower them to do their best work? Or, do you fall into the trap of educational hierarchy? In your setting, what can you do to empower others to do their best work for students and for your school?

After graduation, Sarah and I moved back to Oregon and I quickly started looking for coaching jobs. Although I was not in a teaching position that first year, I knew one of the best ways to get my foot in the door with a school was through coaching. I was blessed to be given the opportunity to join the staff of another Hall of Fame coach at Newberg High School. After a year as the varsity assistant, I was given my first head coaching job as the junior varsity head coach. I was ready. This was going to be my time to shine and prove that I was ready to 'call my own timeouts' as one of my mentors once said. After spending two years as JV head coach, the varsity job became available, and to my surprise, I was offered the position. I could not believe it! At only 25-years-old, I was a varsity head coach!

As I started out on my head coaching journey, my priority was wins on the scoreboard. Just like I had chased personal job titles that I felt equated to success and status, I believed my value and worth as a coach would be evident by winning games, which would lead to winning league and state titles. Whenever you see successful coaches recognized and honored, the first statistic mentioned is their winning percentage. So in my mind, I needed to win more games than I lost in order for others to consider me as successful.

If that is the definition of success for coaches, then I am a failure. After six seasons as a varsity head coach, my overall coaching record, including playoffs, is 73-76. That's right. I have lost more games than I have won, so by the standards I had set for myself when I began my coaching journey, I am a failure. As much as I would love to say that I have a winning record with multiple league and state titles, that is not the reality. However, as I look back and reflect on the past six years of coaching, I can proudly and boldly say that I have in fact been very successful.

I have since learned that as a head coach, my success is not dependent on how many games I win. My success depends on the life-long success of my players once they leave my program. My success depends on the impact I am able to make on the lives of the young people that I am privileged and blessed enough to be able to coach. Do I want to win games? Absolutely! But more than winning games, I want to win lives!

When I took the head coaching job, I told my athletic director and the hiring committee that I would build the program on the foundation of five core principles: *Play Hard, Play Smart, Play Fair, Play Together, Have Fun.* Initially, I thought that if I could implement these five principles that it would lead to winning games and titles. Although it did help make our teams more competitive on the court, what I quickly realized is that the lessons learned were more connected to preparing our players to be successful off the court. All of the lessons we learned while dealing with adversity on the court, or celebrating the success we had on the court, could be connected to lessons outside the lines. Over the past couple of years, I have started telling my players that winning games does not make me proud. What makes me proud is how we play the game, how we act and behave, and who we are as individuals. I teach them that if we play the game the right way by giving our best effort, and if we act and behave appropriately, then we will put ourselves in a position to be successful on the court. We talk with our players about how to behave when they are out in public. Before we get off the bus at a restaurant or grocery

CHOOSE TO BE YOU

store, we remind them they are representing not only themselves with their behavior, but that they are also representing their team, their school, our community, and their family. Our players know that the expectation after a game is that we clear our bench of all trash because it is not the custodial staff or game-management crew's responsibility to clean up after us. It is our responsibility to clean up after ourselves. When we leave a visiting locker room or get off the bus after a game, we make sure that there is no trash left behind. By teaching and training our players to always do the right thing no matter what the situation is in life, we are preparing them for life when they will be in situations on their own and will need to make decisions about behaving in a way that is respectful and responsible. When they are faced with a situation on the court that tests their patience or their judgement in responding in the heat of the moment, they are better prepared to act and behave appropriately and with respect.

I finally understood what it meant to win lives and fully realized what successful coaching looked like this past summer. I had the privilege of attending a former player's wedding. At first, I was more shocked that one of my players was old enough to be getting married. But on the day of the wedding, my world was turned upside down as I sat there during the ceremony and watched as one of my players pledged his love and committed his life to his wife. As the wedding party began entering the reception hall, the groom's parents and grandparents came and sat down at my table. I was humbled that I had been assigned to sit with my player's family. As the night went on, I was able to connect and catch up with several of my former players and their families. As I stood and watched them dance and enjoy the evening, I could not stop thinking about the fact that just a few years earlier, I was coaching them in high school basketball games. What was extra special about this group was

that they were my first group of seniors when I became a head coach for the first time. And now, here we were, five years later, celebrating one of life's biggest and happiest moments together. This was a night I will never forget, and a night that greatly impacted my understanding of the significance and importance of the role we play as coaches and educators.

Later that summer I was able to host a fundraiser 3-on-3 basketball tournament for one of my former players who was battling bone cancer. He had helped as an assistant coach all season long while he took a break from college and went through cancer treatment, but as the bills continued to pile up, we decided to host a tournament with all of the proceeds going towards supporting his  family with medical costs. Just three years earlier, he was a first-team all league basketball player for me. Now, he was literally fighting for his life one day at a time.

For the first part of my career, I was chasing the wrong titles. Both as an educator and a coach, I believed that my success was determined by the title of my position or the banners we would hang in the gym. I now understand that my success is determined by the titles my students and players achieve after they have left the classroom and the court. My success comes through titles such as employee, husband, wife, father, mother, volunteer, survivor, social justice advocate, etc... As educators, we are not in the business of chasing our own titles, rather the future titles our students will someday own. The titles they achieve and earn will be based on the type of people we help them become.

Our job is to prepare our students to be successful after they have left our care, in whatever ways their passions lead them.

Our success is based on their success as humans in their families, their jobs, and as positive contributors to the communities they live in.

To *Choose To Be You* means focusing on doing whatever we can to positively impact those around us and supporting others in becoming their best selves. By doing this, we prepare others for a life of success and whatever title they achieve is a mark of our success, regardless of who knows it. It is not at all about recognition for us, but all about chasing titles and recognition for them. Keep chasing titles!

GUT CHECK
As an **individual**, what title(s) do you wear? Who helped you earn those title(s) and how?

As a **learner**, what lessons are you learning through school or co-curricular activities that will translate into helping you be successful in the next chapter of your life?

As an **educator**, are you more focused on chasing your own titles, or the titles of your students? What titles do your past students hold that make you proud to have had an impact on their life and their story?

CHAPTER

NINE

MAN IN THE MIRROR

So many people in our communities today are battling mental health challenges. For a long time I allowed the stigma of mental health to hold power over how I viewed mental health in general, as well as how I viewed people who I knew suffered from these challenges. In a weird way, I was proud that people viewed me as someone who probably did not struggle with mental illness. The irony came over the past few years as our high school opened a Wellness Center on our campus. Our Wellness Center is an amazing resource for students and families. It is designed to support students through on-site therapists, offering training and classes to students and families, and providing access to multiple community resources to support any type of basic need that students may have. I was able to be a part of the team that made this a reality, and was recently invited to serve on the Community Wellness Collective Governance Board, which runs and operates the Newberg High School Wellness Center. However, as I started to get more involved and even as I began to be a vocal advocate for the work happening down in the Wellness Center by encouraging students to access the available resources, I was conflicted because I was encouraging others to do something that I myself had not done. I had not yet become vulnerable enough with myself to get to the point where I was ready to face my own mental health challenges. On the outside, I was boldly advocating for de-stigmatizing mental health and encouraging those who struggle with mental illness to get support, but was hiding behind my self-made status of an "I've got it all together adult."

As I started to look at myself in the mirror, I realized that I was doing everything within my power to show people who I wanted them to see, instead of boldy and vulnerably living as who I am. One of my favorite songs is 'Man In The Mirror' by Michael Jackson. It, along with 'This Is Me' by Keala Settles, 'Whatever It Takes' by Imagine Dragons, 'Dream Big' by Ryan Shupe and the Rubberband, and 'Don't Stop Believing' by Journey are what make up my daily playlist that I listen to every single morning to remind me about what my mission and motivation is as an educator and as a person. The chorus of 'Man In The Mirror' reads,

I'm starting with the man in the mirror
I'm asking him to change his ways
And no message could have been any clearer
If you want to make the world a better place
Take a look at yourself, and then make a change

As I listen to this each morning, I am reminded that my first responsibility as both an educator and as a person is to *Choose To Be Me*. Before I am able to make a positive impact on the lives of others, it first starts with looking in the mirror and checking to make sure that I am choosing to be the best version of me.

As you may have realized, I am someone who needs tangible reminders. Just like the penny I keep in my pocket to remind me about the importance of relationships and being connected to others, I decided I needed a tangible reminder for how I expect myself to act and behave, as the best version of me in order to build and maintain those relationships with honesty and transparency. Earlier this past school year, our school participated in 'Socktober' with the amazing organization *Skate For Change*. Through this initiative, we were challenged to raise and collect as many pairs of socks possible and then distribute them to people in need within our community. What we learned was that socks are one of the most needed items in homeless shelters throughout the United States. Additionally, the number one cause of sickness and death amongst homeless people in Oregon is hypothermia, which can be protected against by keeping your feet and other extremities warm. The idea behind 'Socktober' was to collect and distribute socks to homeless people as they prepare for the cold months of winter.

As I sat with two students to brainstorm ideas for how to get the student body excited about Socktober, the conversation quickly went to what types of incentives we could offer. We tossed around a few different ideas, but nothing seemed overly exciting. Then out of the blue, one of them asked, "Would you get a tattoo if we reached a certain number of socks collected?" What was likely humor at first thought caused me to pause and think. When I responded with, "Sure.", both students were shocked! I agreed to a tattoo if we collected enough socks for the entire student body. That totalled 1,386 pairs.

As we started the 'Socktober' campaign, socks slowly trickled in. I wasn't sure if we were going to reach our goal. But by the end of October our school raised well over the 1,386 pairs of socks goal. We held a competition for students to submit tattoo designs. The design that gained the most support was the word 'ROAR' across my forehead. We are the Tigers and end our daily announcements, with a school-wide roar. I vetoed that idea for obvious reasons.

I really wanted this tattoo to be something special, something with long term meaning and impact. I also wanted it to be something that represented a part of my life along with being something that I could share with my students and use to inspire and encourage them.

It is crazy how this all happened, but the timing of me being "forced" into getting this tattoo could not have been more perfect. As I wrestled with the thought of which tattoo to get, I was also at the turning point personally where I was actively making the decision to win back my life and choosing to finally start living the *Choose To Be You* lifestyle that I always wanted. For the first time in 14 years, I was facing my anorexia head on. Through all of this, the message of *Choose To Be You* was beginning to take shape.

It was an exciting and scary time. I was on an emotional rollercoaster of being excited and pumped up to be on the path to emotional and mental wellness, but at the same time I was having to unpack and process through my mental illness of anorexia in ways that I had never experienced before.

Addressing your own mental health challenges is not easy. It is difficult, confusing, frustrating, and sometimes embarrassing. I often found myself thinking 'What's wrong with me' or 'Why did this happen to me.' My thoughts were complicated by the fact that I suffer from anorexia, which I had always believed was an issue men didn't face. I was embarrassed to think and accept the fact that I, as a male, had an eating disorder. By seeking out professional help from a counselor and then inviting the people closest to me into my story, I began to find healing and peace. I definitely don't have it all figured out and I know that I will always battle the challenges that come with being anorexic, but I am better today than I was yesterday, and I am surrounded by people who love me and support me every step of the way. That is what counseling has done for me and will continue to do.

The biggest barrier to getting help is usually ourselves.

I know that I hesitated to take the first step and reach out to someone. But once I did, I was so thankful and it has literally changed my life in so many positive ways. What I came to realize and understand is that going to counseling is not a sign of weakness, but it is one of the most courageous decisions that an individual can make. Going to counseling is not about fixing what is wrong with you, it is about seeking help to become the best version of yourself that you are capable of being.

It finally hit me. I was listening to my morning playlist and the song 'Man In The Mirror' came on. I was reminded that before I can make an impact on someone else's life, I had to first start with me, the person who I had to face in the mirror each morning. I instantly knew what my tattoo was going to be! To make sure that I would have a daily reminder about the life that I knew I wanted and needed, I decided I was going to get *Be Who You Is* tattooed on my chest, over my heart. But I wanted it to be even more than that. I decided I would get it done in my handwriting to serve as a reminder that this was more than just a message or slogan, but that it was a message from myself to me. And, it would be tattooed backwards so that as I looked in the mirror each morning, the reflection would be a clear message reminding me to *Be Who You Is*.

Be Who You Is comes from my favorite quote, which I learned from my college basketball coach. He often referenced the quote when teaching students and players about the importance of staying true to who you at your core. I remember the first time I heard my coach say it. I was confused, but intrigued. I think subconsciously when I first heard it, my heart knew that this was the message that would change my life forever. However, at the time, I was not in a place to be ready to make the choice to love and accept myself for who I am.

As I became more aware of my battle with anorexia and started to face the reality of my mental illness, the phrase of *Be Who You Is* kept me moving forward. It gave me personal strength and purpose on a daily basis. I am not sure why this quote spoke so powerfully to me, but it is something I reminded myself of daily, and something that has literally changed my life forever.

I kept my decision about the tattoo a secret from my students and actively worked to put a plan in place that would allow for me to get the tattoo done on campus during an all school assembly. I reached out to our local tattoo shop and the owner worked with me to get a permit from the state that would allow him to do the tattoo at our school. I brainstormed the idea with our Wellness Center co-founder, Kristen Stoller, and she was all on-board to collaborate on a Mental Health Awareness Assembly that we would host in May during Mental Health Awareness Month. During the assembly, we were planning to share ideas and resources about what is available through the Wellness Center and how students can actively focus on taking care of their mental health. As part of the assembly, I was planning to share my story with anorexia along with the message of *Choose To Be You*. After speaking to the student body, I was going to get the tattoo done in the middle of the gym in front of all 1400 students! I was both super excited and super nervous, but I was ready! And then... COVID-19 hit and on March 13, 2020, all schools were closed for what would end up being the rest of the school year.

I wasn't sure what to do. I thought about waiting until the following fall and planning to do my tattoo on campus then. I wanted to keep my promise to this group of students and wanted to find a way to get my tattoo before the end of the school year.

The tattoo shop was closed due to the state-wide mandate. As I waited to hear about it reopening, I connected back with Kristen from the Wellness Center and we decided to make the Mental Health Awareness Assembly happen. We reached out to several community members to collect video messages of positivity and encouragement that we could use for the 'In This Together Virtual Mental Health Awareness Assembly.' We would co-host a Facebook Live event where we would talk about the resources available to students through the Wellness Center. We would share the videos we collected to encourage students, along with helping to promote activities and techniques students could use during the school closure to maintain and work on their mental wellness. As part of the virtual assembly, we decided we would share part of our story and why the conversation around mental health was so important to us.

The day before we were scheduled to host our assembly, I heard from the tattoo shop that they were reopening and I was able to make an appointment. During the virtual assembly, as I told my story, I was able to tell the students that I was scheduled for a tattoo appointment the following week. It wasn't exactly the plan we had, but it was perfect timing nonetheless.

I was happy to be able to fulfil the promise I had made to my students but more so to have my tattoo as a daily reminder to myself. As I look in the mirror, it serves as a sense of motivation and encouragement each morning, and provides a great opportunity for reflection and at the end of the day. Although I am not perfect and may not always live up to the standards I have set for myself, I am constantly reminded that no matter what happens outside of my control, I challenge myself to give my best effort in choosing to be the best version of the man I see in the mirror everyday.

CHAPTER

TEN

JUST DANCE

I will never forget my first exposure to Jostens Renaissance. My Jostens rep invited me to take a group of students to the Renaissance tour stop with Mike Smith and Dr. Phillip Campbell. I had no idea what I was getting into, but I never turned down the opportunity to take students on a field trip. When we got off the bus, we were welcomed by students who were dressed up, holding signs, and having a dance party in the parking lot. It wasn't what we expected to see. As we got closer to the gym where everyone was gathering, we realized that what we experienced outside was nothing compared to what was happening inside. Music was blaring, people were dancing, and everyone was acting like they were at the party of the year! I had never seen anything like this at a school event. My students were excited. A few of them headed straight for the dance party while the rest of us found somewhere to sit.

There were close to 1000 students and educators piled into the bleachers. After some general welcome and introductions, Mike Smith got on the microphone and the first thing he did was ask all of the educators to join him down on the gym floor. I was hesitant, but knew there was no way to avoid it, so I made my way down from the top of the bleachers and stood on the gym floor with all of the other educators. Once we were all down on the gym floor with him, he told us that we were going to participate in a dance challenge and that the students were going to be the judges of who would be named the winner.

I froze! If there is one thing you need to know about me, it is that Mark Brown does NOT dance! In high school, I only went to one high school dance, and the only reason I went was because my now wife invited me to her senior prom. At that prom, I only danced to one song and it was the slow dance. Can you even call that dancing? All I did was sway slowly from side to side. Besides that, I have never danced in public, not even at my own wedding! Seriously, I DO NOT DANCE!

As I stood there frozen in place, I tried to come up with any excuse possible for how I could escape from being down on that gym floor. I realized quickly that was not an option. My shock quickly turned to anger. I was furious that they were making us participate by dancing in front of everyone. Although I was experiencing intense anger and anticipated embarrassment, there was no time for me to process through all of it. The music turned on and I had no other option but to start dancing. I slowly worked to make my way towards the back of the group, but there was no hiding. As I looked up in the bleachers, every single student was standing up with their phone out, smiling and laughing with excitement, watching their teachers and advisors dance. They were absolutely loving it. As I unenthusiastically moved my body while the music played, I looked up and saw all of the students from my school with their phones pointed directly at me, smiling, laughing, and waving while I swayed back and forth. I did not make it very far in the competition and was excused to return to my seat up in the bleachers.

As I sat there in the middle of my students, I was still fuming with anger that stemmed from embarrassment. Up until that moment, I had never danced in public because I was not confident in my abilities as a dancer. To cope with my lack of confidence, I felt it was better to avoid embarrassment by never making myself vulnerable by way of dancing in front of others. In my mind, if I never danced, I would never be embarrassed, right? But as I sat there and listened to the words of Mike Smith and Dr. Phillip Campbell, something clicked inside of me. It first clicked in my head, but then quickly clicked in my heart as well.

I realized that one of the best ways to connect with students was through making ourselves vulnerable as educators and leaders.

I had always believed that my mission as an educator had more to do with relationships than it did curriculum, but up until this point I struggled to make that the reality in my daily habits. I knew it was supposed to be all about relationships, but I did not know how to make that happen.

My anger and embarrassment slowly started to fade away. Through the stories and inspiration that both Mike and Phillip shared, I instantly knew that my life as an educator and as a person would never again be the same. I could not return to my classroom and continue doing things the way I had always done them now knowing what I knew after listening to the two of them speak. I would be doing wrong by my students, but more importantly I would be doing wrong to myself if I did not make a change.

I had been successful in connecting with students as an educator. I showed interest in them as individuals and supported them beyond just academics. But I had always made sure to present myself in a way that appeared as if my life was perfect and I had it all figured out. I never put myself in situations to be vulnerable with students because I wanted them to see me and respect me for my success without knowing my failures or struggles. I hid most of my personal life from my students and only exposed what I wanted students to see and know about me.

I love the movie 'The Greatest Showman.' It's highly entertaining with wonderful choreography and music. My favorite part is when the circus actors are denied entrance into the fancy reception with all of the rich people. Although the group of performers was used to being rejected and labeled as different, they had begun to find a new sense of confidence in themselves. In response to being denied entrance to the reception, the bearded lady begins singing the song "This Is Me" and the group of actors charge into the ballroom to proclaim to everyone there that they will no longer let the thoughts, words, and judgements of others keep them from being their true, authentic selves. The song "This Is Me" has become the anthem of my life! Read the lyrics, soak in the message of the song:

I am not a stranger to the dark
Hide away, they say
'Cause we don't want your broken parts
I've learned to be ashamed of all my scars
Run away, they say
No one'll love you as you are

But I won't let them break me down to dust
I know that there's a place for us
For we are glorious

When the sharpest words wanna cut me down
I'm gonna send a flood, gonna drown them out
I am brave, I am bruised
I am who I'm meant to be, this is me

Look out 'cause here I come
And I'm marching on to the beat I drum
I'm not scared to be seen
I make no apologies, this is me

Another round of bullets hits my skin
Well, fire away 'cause today, I won't let the shame sink in
We are bursting through the barricades and
Reaching for the sun (we are warriors)
Yeah, that's what we've become (yeah, that's what we've become)

I won't let them break me down to dust

I know that there's a place for us
For we are glorious

When the sharpest words wanna cut me down
I'm gonna send a flood, gonna drown them out
I am brave, I am bruised
I am who I'm meant to be, this is me

Look out 'cause here I come
And I'm marching on to the beat I drum
I'm not scared to be seen
I make no apologies, this is me

This is me
and I know that I deserve your love
'cause there's nothing I'm not worthy of

When the sharpest words wanna cut me down
I'm gonna send a flood, gonna drown them out
This is brave, this is proof
This is who I'm meant to be, this is me

Look out 'cause here I come
And I'm marching on to the beat I drum
I'm not scared to be seen
I make no apologies, this is me

When the sharpest words wanna cut me down
I'm gonna send a flood, gonna drown them out

I'm gonna send a flood
Gonna drown them out

This is me

That is how I want to live my life! Unashamed of who I am and not living by anyone else's standards or expectations but my own! Regardless of what other people say or think, I want to be proud and confident in who I am. I want to wake up each morning, look myself in the mirror, and undoubtedly and unapologetically *Choose To Be Me*. Living this way is not easy. It seems as if the more boldly we live, the more critical others become of us.

I am no longer willing to hide the real me to appease and satisfy the expectations of others. Choosing To Be Me means being able to stand boldly and proclaim 'This Is Me' for anyone and everyone to hear.

As an educator and even more so now as an educational leader, I have a responsibility to model what it means to *Choose To Be Me* for both students and staff. If I am going to proclaim that our primary responsibility as educators is building relationships, which I absolutely believe, then I need to be willing to make myself vulnerable. Vulnerability breeds relationships because vulnerability invites others into the most intimate parts of our lives. By making myself vulnerable with staff and students, I am telling them that I trust them, that I want them to know me fully for who I am, and that I want to in turn support them in being who they are. This is my mission as an educator, and this is exactly who I want to be!

ELEVEN

RENAISSANCE

O nce I recovered from my public dancing debut, I could not stop thinking about what I had seen, heard, and experienced at the Jostens Renaissance tour stop. I kept wondering if it was really possible to have a school that looked and felt like the schools Dr. Phillip Campbell talked about in his presentation. Although initially excited about the possibilities, I was skeptical about being able to recreate the experience in my own school.

Let me tell you a little about my school. We are a one high school town of about 25,000 people. Between our traditional campus and the alternative satellite campus, we have about 1,600 students. We are classified as a 6A high school, which is the largest classification in our state. It's quite unique and special to be such a large school in a one high school town.

When I was hired as a part-time health teacher in 2012, our high school was divided into four small schools: Blue School, Green School, Silver School, and Yellow School. Each small school had its own principal, counselor, secretary, and teaching staff. When ninth-grade students entered the high school, they forecasted for which small school they wanted to join. It was a lottery system, with most students getting their first choice. Each school held their own staff meetings, conducted their own school-specific assemblies, and had an established culture that separated them from the other three small schools.

Although there were four separate small schools, all students still graduated with a Newberg High School diploma. All athletics and activities, such as band, choir, orchestra, etc. were inclusive of all students from each of the small schools as were electives and other non-core classes. As a Health teacher, I always had students in my classes from all four small schools.

In the middle of my second year of teaching, our superintendent announced that we would be transitioning away from small schools and back into a comprehensive high school. As a younger teacher who had not been at the school very long, along with the fact that I taught and coached students from all four small schools, I didn't think too much about it. At the time, it didn't seem to have that big of an impact on me.

In the spring of that school year, my athletic director called me into a closed door meeting to tell me that as we transitioned away from small schools, there were going to be some reductions to our staffing. As a second year probationary teacher on a temporary contract, my position was being eliminated. I was crushed. This was the school and the community that I wanted to be in. I had envisioned spending my entire career here. But as things stood in that moment, I would be without a job at the end of the school year.

Much to my surprise, in the weeks following that meeting, I was presented with an opportunity to stay at the high school. They were looking for a new Activities Director. It was not a full-time position, but it would keep me in the school and the community where I wanted to be. It ended up being a .33 FTE job. That's right. A .33 Activities Director position. Any high school educator reading this is probably laughing to themselves at the thought of accepting that job. Luckily for me, I was ignorant to what an Activities Director's responsibilities were and was desperate to stay. I accepted the position.

CHOOSE TO BE YOU

That same spring, I interviewed for the Varsity Boys Basketball position and was offered the job. Needless to say, it was a busy spring and summer, and I definitely had my hands full. Admittedly, the best part about it was that I had no idea what I was in for!

As we started planning for the school year, I quickly came to realize and understand the challenges that were ahead of us. During one of our first meetings as a full Associated Student Body (ASB) student leadership group, we started talking about our plans for homecoming, and I noticed an increased tension throughout the room. All of the students started talking about the 'traditions' and activities that had become customary within their small schools over the past few years. As they shared ideas, many of the students became defensive when their small school's event or activity was not immediately accepted by the rest of the group. It's almost as if it had quickly turned into a competition to prove to the rest of the group that their small school's ideas and activities were better than the others. It was an uneasy and almost unnerving feeling for me. I was quickly realizing that this 'job' was going to be much more difficult than I had originally anticipated. Not only was it new to me, but this situation was new to our whole school. The actions we took and the decision we would make as a student leadership group over the course of the upcoming school year would be vitally important and impactful in creating our 'new' school culture. Coming out of the small school model and reunifying our high school into a single, comprehensive school, we had a gloriously scary task ahead of us. Looking back on it now as a more seasoned and experienced educator, it's exciting to think about what that situation and opportunity could be like today, knowing what I know now about school climate and culture. At the time, it was intimidating, overwhelming, and one of the greatest professional challenges I have ever faced.

As the school year went on, the conflict continued. Every milestone event or major decision brought conflict and posturing resulting from the small school mentality and allegiances that students had. Don't get me wrong, this was an amazing group of students I was privileged to be working with! They were dedicated, hard working, and passionate about making it a great school year for their peers. That group taught me so much about leadership and working collaboratively. I will always remember those individual students and how they helped shape who I am as an educator and as a leader today.

As we worked through the struggles and challenges of unifying our school, we quickly learned that we would be much more successful if we could create a new identity and rally cry for people to get behind and excited about. This was an important realization for me as a leader. When making change, instead of putting all of your focus and energy into overcoming the old and convincing people that the new is better than the old, it is best to honor the old while creating and generating positive-centered focus moving forward. I have seen many change initiatives fail or struggle to gain support because the leadership has worked so hard to convince people why the new is better than old. This causes people to believe or perceive that there was something wrong with the old, which can be very painful, embarrassing, and disrespectful to those who found comfort and pride in it. I believe it is best to promote positive energy on the new, while also acknowledging and respecting the old. For us, in our situation, we had to learn to stop fighting the old small school ideals and mentality, and instead find ways to generate excitement for the new idea of being a comprehensive high school. Once we were able to flip that perspective for ourselves, it became much easier to generate excitement and buy-in from everyone else in the school community.

This was the birth of *Newberg Nation*. If you didn't know the back story, but spent any time around Newberg High School today, you would have never guessed that *Newberg Nation* was only just a few years old. As we worked to create a rally cry and generate positive momentum moving forward, we came up with the *Newberg Nation*. Not only was this a new identity for people to grasp onto and embrace, it also created a bridge from the small school era into our new situation as a comprehensive high school. It didn't matter which small school a student, educator, or parent had been associated with because we were all now a part of something new. We branded *Newberg Nation* all over the place with shirts, flags, chants, and cheers. We even started using social media and created a *Newberg Nation* Instagram page.

Tangent Rant: If you are an educator and not involved on a social media platform, you are missing out on daily professional development. Over the past few years, I have become more and more active on social media, and it is by far the best source of inspiration and motivation for me as an educator. I get to connect with some of the most innovative, creative, and amazing educators from all over the world each and every day. My PLN (professional learning network) is my most used resource when dealing with a situation as an administrator or needing to generate ideas for our school. I feel incredibly blessed to be connected with so many outstanding educators who encourage me each and every day to be better!

I fought being involved on social media for a long time. I quickly realized however, that social media is where our students are spending a lot of their time. Social media platforms will change over time, but social media is here to stay. Rather than fighting it, I have learned that it is better to embrace it and be active on it.

I remember Dr. Phillip Campbell once telling me about 'disrupting the feed.' I think a lot of adults have a negative view of social media because we have heard the horror stories about bullying and confrontations that stem from it. He challenges us as educators to use our influence to disrupt feeds by creating positivity and posts that encourage those who see it. Students want to get a sneak peek into the lives of their educators. They desire to know what we are like outside the four walls of our school house. Social media is a way to continue making the positive impact and influence that all educators desire to have on students even when they are not at school. Instead of fighting it, I encourage you to embrace it and get involved in being a #FeedDisruptor. If you are new to social media, I encourage you to set up an account and then reach out to me. My Twitter and Instagram handle is @HeyMarkBrown. You can also find me on Facebook. I will be happy to connect you with my amazing PLN of #RockStar educators!

Social media is one of the greatest tools and resources available to schools to help create your school's culture and identity! As my good friend Dr. Darrin M. Peppard says it: "Be the author of your story." Darrin promotes the idea that if we are not the ones telling the story of what happens within the walls of our school, someone else will. And we probably won't like their version! As educators, we all know that there are so many amazing and powerful things that happen on a daily basis. Through the use of social media, you have the opportunity and ability to tell your school's story and invite your community to see what really happens inside our classrooms and hallways. You can create hashtags for students to follow and campaigns for your community to participate in. Social media is a great way to highlight the accomplishments of individuals and groups across your campus. Just like how students would cut out articles from the local newspaper that talked about their team's win or award they were presented with, they now 'like' and 'share' posts on social media. When I take photos at school and ask students if I can post it on the school's social media pages, they love it! It is such a simple way to make someone's day while spreading positivity and articulating the story of your school to your community. *Tangent Rant over.*

Newberg Nation took off and was a huge success! As an ASB student leadership group, we finally felt like we were making progress towards creating a healthy and positive school culture. As we continued making more posts on social media about various events and activities, complaints began to arise. They were mostly from groups and individuals who were frustrated that the majority of our posts were centered around what was happening in athletics. I can't say they were wrong. Though I was initially put off by the comments, I realized that we were in fact highlighting the sports teams and their events and achievements more than any other activity. We started to do a better job of highlighting performing arts, but that was about it. We were still primarily focused on athletics and using sporting events to brand *Newberg Nation* and bring people together. It was working, but it was a very limited and narrow focus.

If you remember from Chapter 10, I had mixed feelings about Jostens Renaissance after my first exposure during their tour stop. However, once I got past the shame and humiliation from dancing in public, I quickly realized that Renaissance is exactly what my school needed. I believe that if we could find a way to bring Renaissance to our campus, it had the potential to completely transform our school culture. As mentioned earlier, I was skeptical at the idea of being able to create the type of climate and culture within our school that Dr. Phillip Campbell talked about that day during the tour stop. But, I was ready to dive in and give it a try!

I was given the opportunity by my principal to attend the Jostens Renaissance National Conference (JRNC) that summer and one of the first things I picked up on was the Renaissance formula of the five R's:

RESPECT

RECOGNIZE

REWARD

+ REINFORCE

RESULTS

It seemed like almost every single breakout session I went to spoke to the importance and the power of this formula. It seemed so simple, yet came with more data than you can imagine to prove that it works. If you want practical ideas about how to implement Renaissance and this formula on your campus, I strongly encourage you to check out my good friend Steve Bollar's, a.k.a *Stand Tall Steve*, book, Ideas, Ideas, Ideas. It is jammed packed with ideas to make your campus come alive with energy and excitement! It is the perfect roadmap for anyone looking to use the Five R's formula to create a more positive, engaging, and inclusive school climate and culture.

I think I hooked on to the Five R's formula so quickly because, to me, it perfectly aligned with the message of *Choose To Be You*. As schools, once we identify what it is that we Respect, if we then find ways to Recognize, Reward, and continually Reinforce those habits and actions amongst students and staffulty, then we will get the positive Results that we want. As individuals, if we Respect ourselves and who we are, and then Recognize, Reward, and continually Reinforce our success in loving ourselves and living as our best authentic self, then we will see positive Results of living life with courage by being able to boldly proclaiming to the world that THIS IS ME.

As school communities, implementing the Five R's formulas is all about encouraging your students and staffulty to embrace the call to *Choose To Be You.* Jostens Renaissance is all about encouraging everyone on your campus to live life as their best selves, while making a positive impact on those around them. It doesn't matter what you are passionate about or what your skill-set is. As long as you give your best effort to be true to yourself, and strive to make a positive impact on those around you, you deserve to be recognized and celebrated. Jostens Renaissance helps create a framework for Recognizing, Rewarding, and Reinforcing the positive attributes and traits of EVERYONE on your campus. When we do that, we create school climates and cultures that are positive, inclusive, and engaging. We create schools where everyone feels like they belong. It takes our schools from a place where students and staffulty have to be, to the place where they want to be! Like Dr. Phillip Campbell says, when people feel seen, heard, and loved, it changes everything about how they live their life. There is actually a group of Renaissance educators who have been lobbying to add a sixth R to the formula: Relationships. But regardless of whether or not it actually gets added, we all know that Relationships is at the root of everything we do within Renaissance schools.

By implementing the Jostens Renaissance framework and philosophy, school leaders are proclaiming that above everything else we do within our schools, Relationships must be our top priority! If we want students to learn, we must love them. If we want staffulty to be at their best for students, we must love them. This is the power of Renaissance, and this is the power of *Choose To Be You.*

Above everything else, we must learn to love ourselves, love others, and encourage others to love themselves!

When we started to implement the Five R's on our campus, everything about *Newberg Nation* changed. We were able to create a more inclusive and all-encompassing culture that highlighted and prioritized all groups across our campus. It did not matter if you were an athlete, a thespian, an art student, involved with FFA, or an outstanding academic student. We

CHOOSE TO BE YOU

started to send a powerful message that everyone on our campus mattered, and we started finding ways to highlight all individuals and groups throughout. We are always looking for new ways to increase recognition for students and staffulty. Just as we as individuals are constantly a work in progress as we embrace the call to *Choose To Be You,* our schools are constantly a work in progress as well. We will never get to the point where we 'have arrived.' We need to continue working to be better, each and every day, as both individuals and as schools.

GUT CHECK

As an **individual**, what are you doing to be better each and every day? What can/should you focus on starting today to help you focus on embracing the call to *Choose To Be You?*

As a **learner**, what are you passionate about? What are you interested in and how do you like to spend your time at school? Does your school value your passion? Do you see the Five R's formula actively and intentionally implemented throughout your campus? If not, what can you do to help bring this formula to your campus?

As an **educator**, do you prioritize Relationships above everything else on your campus? What can you do to either bring or enhance the Five R's formula to your campus? How can you help Recognize, Reward, and Reinforce what you and your school Respects, so that you help bring positive Results to your school?

CHAPTER

TWELVE

BETTER TOGETHER

*T*his will be a very short chapter, but a very important one.

As we started to implement Renaissance and the Five R's formula on our campus, I was not my best self for my school as a leader. I had gone to JRNC by myself and felt like I was the only person on our campus who truly understood what Renaissance was all about. Instead of reaching out and bringing others into the brainstorming and planning, I tried doing it all on my own. We had some great success those first few years. We started recognizing students and staffulty of the month, had a huge end-of-year academic awards celebration, a school-wide talent show, and did several other things that helped shape and impact our school climate and culture in positive ways. But I was doing almost all of this work by myself, and it was my own fault. As really the only person making decisions and implementing strategies, people started to recognize what I was doing and were extremely complimentary. As someone who struggles with being a people pleaser and wants approval of others, I liked this! People were seeing my hard work and were giving me credit for a lot of our success as a school. This motivated me to do even more, but for all of the wrong reasons.

I picked up a copy of Mike Smith's <u>Legacy vs. Likes</u> book. As I read his words, it was as though he was speaking directly to me. In all honesty, that book was a major turning point for me not only as an educator, but also as an individual and someone who struggles with mental illness that is connected to self-worth and self-concept. As one who has spent the majority of my life chasing an identity that I thought people would approve of, I realized that I was more concerned with likes than I was my legacy. Mike helped me understand the power of legacy and how my success as an individual is rooted and found in the success of others.

As a leader, my achievements and accomplishments are not based on what I do, but by what I am able to empower others to do.

My success is the success of my students. It is the success of my staffulty. The true power of Renaissance is found in collective efficacy and collaboration, with a focus on highlighting others in any and every way possible. I learned and realized that the best way to help my school become like the schools I heard Dr. Phillip Campbell talk about that day on the tour stop was through establishing a culture of shared responsibility and ownership. My work as an individual might make a small, immediate, and noticeable impact. But the only way to ensure that we truly develop the climate and culture that I so desperately desired, and one that would last long beyond my time at the school, was through sharing the work and empowering others. Renaissance is meant to be shared and owned by everyone on your campus. It is not yours.

Climate and culture are not tied to individuals. They are the reflection of everyone within the organization.

Therefore, in order to create a positive climate and culture, it must include everyone taking action and being involved.

The best thing that happened to me and to our school was forming our WOW committee. After two colleagues, Angela Kantz and Kaylee Tolley, attended a

Jostens Renaissance educator workshop with me, they finally saw and understood what I had been exposed to over the past few years, and they could not wait to get more involved. They started brainstorming on their own, and even organized regular WOW committee meetings where the three of us would plan and strategize for whatever was coming next on our Renaissance journey. All of a sudden, everything we did was bigger and better than ever before! Angela and Kaylee transformed our hallways and brought our school to life with decor and tangible reminders. They found new and unique ways to highlight groups and

helped bring more attention to the already great things happening around campus! They brought others into the work and started to create a collective group of educators who are on-fire for making our school the best that it could be! But most of all, they taught me that our work as educators is best when it is shared with others. I look forward every week to our regular WOW committee meetings.

I joke with Angela and Kaylee that these are the most expensive meetings I have because they always involve asking for funds for our next project! But in all honesty, they are the highlight of my week. We share a passion and energy for cultivating a positive school climate and culture. That is how Renaissance is designed to work! With the mindset that we are always *better together*!

GUT CHECK

As an **individual**, do you live life more concerned about the legacy you are creating, or about the likes you receive from others?

As a **learner**, when was a time that you remember experiencing the power of Better Together?

As an **educator**, are you regularly collaborating with other educators across your campus? Do you collaborate with educators outside of your department? If not, what is keeping you from reaching out and connecting with other educators? If you are, what have been the results of that collaboration? How can you build on those results to make an even bigger and better impact on your school?

CHAPTER

THIRTEEN

GROWING PAINS

One of the best lessons I have learned is that it is better to be proactive in how we choose to live our lives as opposed to being reactive in the choices we make based on the events that happen in our lives. When we live a proactive life, we claim that we are in control of who we are and how we live. When we live a reactive life, we let the pressures of the world around us dictate who we are and impact the decisions that we make.

One thing that has really helped me in understanding this concept is the equation of E+R=O. This comes from the Focus 3 organization and has been powerful in helping me put this concept of living proactively instead of reactively into practice in my life. When spelled out, the equations stands for Experience +

Response = Outcome. All throughout life, we will encounter various experiences that are outside of our control. Whether the experience is positive or negative, the outcome that we will receive is based upon our response to the experience. When something bad happens, the outcome does not have to be negative. When something good happens, the outcome is not automatically positive. As individuals, we have power and choice in helping to determine the outcome of every experience that we encounter. When we choose to live proactively by choosing to be the best version of ourselves and who we are at our core, we are much more likely to be prepared to respond responsibly to whatever good or bad experience comes our way. People who live more reactive to situations and who are not confident in who they are at their core are more likely to struggle to achieve positive outcomes when faced with experiences that are outside of their control. They will be more tempted to respond to the situation based on emotions they are experiencing in the moment rather than out of wisdom and confidence in who they are at their core. That's what I did for the majority of my life. My response to experiences was based out of fear, guilt, shame, and a desire to control the experience, rather than focusing on controlling the outcome based on how I responded. Although my anorexia is an eating disorder, my counselor has helped me learn and understand that it will take anything that it can grab onto in my life to convince me that I am not good enough and create more feelings of guilt and shame that are unrelated to eating. Our mind is an incredibly powerful tool that we must learn to manage and use responsibly by living proactively as opposed to reactively.

As you know by now, I need tangible reminders to proactively put what I have learned into practice. One thing that has really helped me is by putting the $E+R=O$ equation above my office door. It is a visual reminder to me that no matter what experience or situation comes  through my office door, the outcome is going to be based largely off of my response to the situation. Likewise, every time I leave my office to head out into the hallways and classrooms, I have no idea what I am about to walk into. So, I had better be prepared to respond with a healthy, calm, and proactive approach. One of the great things about being a school administrator is that no day is like another! There is no telling what is going to happen on a given day, and a lot of what we deal with is unlike anything we have ever dealt with before. It is important to remember that regardless of what happens outside of my control, whether good or bad, I have power to influence the outcome based on how I choose to respond to the experience.

It is important to understand that although we have the power to influence the outcome based on how we choose to respond to a situation, we still do not have absolute power to control every situation we will face. Throughout life, we will all experience growing pains. Although growing pains are not always fun in the moment, they are an incredibly powerful part of our journey in learning what it means to *Choose To Be You*.

At only 5'5" tall, I didn't have any major growth spurts or have to experience too many physical growing pains. There was one point in my life in second-grade where my knees bothered me quite a bit, but nothing too serious and it did not last long. While I cannot say that I understand physical growing pains, I most definitely understand emotional ones.

My first job out of college was at a challenge course as a manager. I had worked as a course facilitator during the summers through high school and college. I love the power of experiential learning and often miss my days climbing trees and hanging out in the woods!

As a facilitator, I often worked with groups and talked about the difference between our "Comfort Zone" and our "Growth Zone." I used to refer to the "Growth Zone" the "Groan Zone" because as we learn and grow, there is often a lot of groaning that comes with it. As humans, we like to stay in our comfort zone. If we are going to learn and grow, we must step outside of our comfort zone and be willing to experience discomfort. The beauty of this is that we expose ourselves to new ideas and new perspectives. It is through these experiences that we are able to expand our understanding of the world and of who we are at our core. When you make the choice to *Choose To Be You*, you commit to constantly learning and growing. It is a decision to accept constant discomfort as you push beyond where you currently are in search of a better understanding of the world around you, and better understanding of who you are. As my publisher, Code Breaker, Inc. says, "It's ok to be where you are. It's not ok to stay there."

Choose To Be You is not a destination, it is a commitment to a life of growing and learning, and a commitment to embracing discomfort.

It is in our discomfort that we find true peace and

beauty. It is in our discomfort that we find who we truly are.

In my battle against anorexia, I have experienced a lot of growing pains. Making the decision to begin the journey towards mental wellness was a difficult decision. I had become extremely comfortable in my anorexia. It was a way of life that I did not ever want to give up. The decision to want to overcome anorexia was the most difficult decision I've ever made. I knew that it would mean choosing to become uncomfortable and choosing to face the deepest and darkest areas of my life head on. Anorexia had become my identity and my comfort zone. Stepping outside of that has been a daily challenge. It has required me to have difficult conversations with those closest to me, and has required me to admit a lot of things that I thought would remain a secret my entire life. The decision to chase mental wellness is a choice that I made, and it is a choice that has brought a lot of growing pains.

The first growing pains came when I told my wife and my parents about my anorexia. Although I knew that they would respond with love and support, it is never easy to admit your shortcomings or your struggles with people who you respect. As a son and a husband, I want my parents and my wife to be proud of me. I want them to look up to me and to admire who I am. Admitting that I struggle with an eating disorder felt like I was admitting I am flawed and inadequate. What I've learned is that when you *Choose To Be You*, it is necessary to surround yourself with people who will love and support you in pursuing your best self. When we become vulnerable with ourselves, we need people around us who will love us unconditionally, and who will help support us in processing through the experience of becoming the best version of ourselves. The initial conversations with Sarah and with my parents were awkward and intimidating, but I am thankful to have people who love me and who choose to walk alongside me in my journey towards mental wellness.

The next growing pain came when I went to my first counseling appointment. I knew that counseling was something I needed. Like many people, I had stigmatized going to counseling and in my mind, going meant that there must be something wrong with me. The idea of going to counseling was not only terrifying, it was also embarrassing. I struggled with the idea that I was so broken and in need of fixing that I had to pay someone to give me advice. That was my perception of counseling and where I was on my journey.

I had told both my wife and my parents that I wanted to go to counseling, but delayed finding a counselor because I just wasn't quite ready for that step. When the day came for my first appointment, I was nervously excited. I was not quite sure what to expect, but it began to feel good to be taking this step towards finding mental wellness and working to improve myself.

My first appointment went great! I made an immediate connection with my counselor and felt confident she would be a good fit to support me in my journey. She provided positive feedback and simple suggestions I could begin implementing into my daily routine. She did a great job of explaining to me that the process of counseling was going to take time because we were literally going to have to undo and rewire parts of my brain. Her explanation made me realize how 'normal' and natural my anorexic tendencies and habits had become. She helped me understand that this journey was not about fixing me, but rather it was about finding, embracing, and loving my true self. She offered me hope, which is something that I had not known for a long time.

The growing pains of counseling started to come after our first few sessions. As my counselor and I got to know each other better and she started to become more aware of my situation and my story, she started to suggest specific tips and tricks that I could try when I was experiencing urges to indulge in my anorexic tendencies. This became painful because it made me that much more aware of how much control anorexia had over every aspect of my life. It started to feel almost overwhelming at times. The growing pains continued when I had to go back to my counselor and talk about the struggles I was experiencing. I wanted to be able to walk into my appointments and tell her how great I was doing and talk about how much success I was experiencing. In order to be honest and really get to the point where I was making true progress towards mental wellness, I had to be honest with her and myself.

This is yet another example of how learning and growing is not easy. When we try new things or work to improve in different areas of our lives, it forces us to get outside of our comfort zone. When we ask for help from others, it can make us feel vulnerable and exposed. As educators and learners, this is a great reminder for us. Learning is not always easy and we may not experience immediate success. It can be messy and frustrating. If we allow others to support us in our learning, and if we persevere through failure and struggle, we give ourselves the opportunity to learn and grow. Asking for help is not a sign of weakness or admitting that you are incapable. Asking for help takes courage and strength, and it is a declaration to others that you desire to grow and be better. The best learning comes with struggles and setbacks. In schools, just like in life, we must be abounding in grace and patience for both others and for ourselves. We cannot push people too hard and too fast, but we also can't give up when things get difficult. Step by step and experience by experience, we must continue to look for opportunities to move forward and continue making progress. Even if our progress is not happening as fast as we would like it to, when we keep at it and allow others to support us in the journey, the growing pains will soon fade away and we will be better, stronger, and more equipped individuals than we were before. That's the beauty of Choosing To Be You.

Our past and our mistakes do not define us.

They play a major role in helping to shape and mold us, but they do not define who we are. When you make the choice to be you, you make the choice to continue learning and growing every single day. There are no days off and there is no destination in the journey to *Choose To Be You.*

GUT CHECK

As a **learner,** what are some examples of emotional and mental growing pains you have experienced? What do you do when you experience growing pains?

As an e**ducator,** what does it look like in your classroom when students or other educators are experiencing growing pains? Do you show up to support them? If so, how? If not, why not?

As an i**ndividual,** who do you reach out to when you are experiencing growing pains? If you do not have people that you connect with regularly for support, who are some people who you can identify as supports and resources that you should begin reaching out to more regularly, especially when you are experiencing growing pains?

FOURTEEN

LET'S TALK ABOUT MENTAL HEALTH

One of my passions as an educator is encouraging, inspiring, and equipping others to actively engage in conversations around mental health. Now, I'll start by saying, it's not easy. The topic of mental health can be intimidating and scary for many people. Historically, we have not done a great job of facilitating this conversation in schools. It has primarily been limited to health classes or something that school counselors talk to students about. Some schools might participate in a Mental Health Awareness week in May during Mental Health Awareness Month, but it is often a small and easily overlooked event. And, when the discussion is brought up, it often leads people to think about mental illnesses like severe depression, schizophrenia, and other diagnosed and treated diseases. Additionally, it almost always ends with a focus on suicide and suicide prevention. We have conditioned students and educators alike to be afraid of the mental health conversations. I think too many people have the opinion that if mental illness is not directly impacting them, then they don't need to spend time talking about it. Unfortunately, the number of people impacted by mental illness continues to rise. According to the National Alliance on Mental Illness (NAMI), 1 in 5 adults in the US experience mental illness, and 17% of youth between the ages of 6-17 experience a mental health disorder[1]. As educators, we can no longer avoid the mental health conversation. It's time we start having the conversation, but we need to make sure we understand how to talk about it. Our students deserve and need it.

One of the first things I always like to help people understand is that mental health is not limited to mental illness and disease. Mental illness and disease are at one end of the mental health spectrum. At the other end of the spectrum is wellness. As humans, we all land somewhere on the spectrum.

We all have mental health.

Just like many of us focus on our physical health by eating healthy food and exercising, we need to be intentional about taking care of our mental health.

Some things we can do to exercise our mental health include journaling, getting physical exercise, creating routines, planning intentional time away from technology, connecting with someone we trust to have intimate conversations with and seek advice from, etc. There are so many simple, yet effective strategies that we can all incorporate into our daily lives. I am not a mental health expert, but I encourage you to think about some of the suggestions I listed above, or find other strategies for exercising your mental health on a regular basis. Regardless of the strategies you choose to utilize, the important thing is being intentional, and then being honest with yourself.

I believe we need to make mental health discussions a regular and ongoing topic of conversation within our schools.

We need to make the conversation about mental health normal.

I think we need to start by focusing on what I just talked about in the previous paragraph: We all have mental health. Students and Staffulty all need to understand this. Now, I want to be very clear that I am not minimizing the seriousness of severe mental illness, disease, and disorders. As someone who struggles with anorexia, I very much understand how serious, dangerous, and real mental illness is. However, if we limit the mental health conversation to diagnosed illness, disease, and disorders, we miss an opportunity to engage everyone in important and critical conversations.

In order to remove the stigma around the mental health conversation and help people understand the importance of focusing on working towards mental wellness, we should pivot the traditional conversation to describe the positive components of mental health. As already mentioned, we need to clearly articulate that everyone has mental health. That means that many people experience mental wellness, which is great! If you are someone who is mentally and emotionally healthy, you still have mental health. I know it seems like a fairly simple concept, but it's probably the first time some of you are thinking about it like this. If this is the first time you are thinking about it, I encourage you to pause in your reading and spend some time processing this concept and analyzing your personal mental health. If you do not spend time regularly journaling, this might be a great time to start! I have found that writing and journaling is one of the best ways to process how I am feeling and how I begin to understand what I am thinking. It might feel awkward at first, but don't worry, it gets easier! Give it a try. You might like it!

As educators, we have the opportunity to impact students during the most formidable and impressionable stages of their lives. According to NAMI, 50% of all lifetime mental illnesses develop by age 14 and 75% develop by age 24[2]. I don't quote those statistics to put pressure on educators and make you feel as though it's your job to prevent this from happening to students. We cannot control who struggles with mental illness and who does not. The more exposed people are to understanding what mental health is and if they understand some of the primary warning signs surrounding mental illness, they are more likely to reach out for help. The earlier that people who struggle with mental health challenges receive support, the less likely it is that their mental health challenges have long term and significant impacts on their life. As educators, the more we are engaging in mental health conversations with students, the more likely they will be able to identify mental health challenges in themselves or their friends, and the more likely they are to begin receiving early professional help.

According to NAMI, there are 10 common warning signs[3] that someone might be experiencing mental health challenges:
• Feeling very sad or withdrawn for more than two weeks

- Seriously trying to harm or kill oneself or making plans to do so
- Sever out-of-control, risk-taking behaviors
  Sudden, overwhelming fear for no reason
  Not eating, throwing up or using laxatives to lose weight; significant weight loss or weight gain
- Seeing, hearing or believing things that are not real
- Repeatedly using drugs or alcohol
- Drastic changes in mood, behavior, personality or sleeping habits
- Extreme difficulty in concentrating or staying still
- Intense worries or fears that get in the way of daily activities

Unfortunately, many have never heard of or seen a list like this. I believe that this is where all educators, all adults, and all students have an opportunity and responsibility to help promote mental health awareness. If people are aware of some of the primary warning signs, they are more likely to take action if they themselves or someone else they know are experiencing any of the signs.

Once people understand the warning signs, it is important that they understand what resources and supports are available. I am a big believer that the first level of support is the people around you. This is another reason why it must be a top priority for educators to focus on building relationships with students, and helping to facilitate relationship building amongst students.

If students feel that they have established and authentic relationships with educators and their peers, they are more likely to reach out for help when they need it.

I can't say it enough: As educators, we must remain focused on and committed to RELATIONSHIPS FIRST!

We must realize that if someone reaches out to us and expresses concerns about their mental health, it does not mean that we are responsible for providing all the answers and support that they need. As a licensed teacher and administrator, I am not a mental health expert. If someone comes to you and reveals information about challenges they are facing that you are not equipped to support them in, you have a responsibility to make sure they get connected with someone who can provide them with the support they need. We need to make an intentional decision for ourselves and communicate with them that we are not equipped to help, but make a commitment to them that we will support them in getting connected with someone who can. There are some great mental health first aid and youth mental health first aid training programs that train people in being able to support those in crisis or who are experiencing mental health challenges. The training is focused around how to engage in positive and supportive conversations, with a priority on connecting the person in need with the next level of help that their situation requires. I encourage schools to look into providing mental health first aid training for both educators and students. The more people on our campuses who are prepared and equipped to support people who are facing mental health challenges, the better!

One suggestion I have for you is to start a wellness committee on your campus. This could be a group of staffulty and students who are committed to helping spread positivity and awareness for mental health. One simple idea would be to start with a #WellnessWednesday campaign. Every Wednesday, your wellness committee makes positive social media posts using the hashtag #WellnessWednesday, as well as creating opportunities for students and staffulty to engage in activities that promote positivity and awareness for the topic of mental health.

One of the most challenging parts of publishing this book was deciding what the cover design was going to be. I went through multiple iterations of cover design options and just couldn't decide what I wanted it to be.

I ended up choosing a much more simple design than I had originally imagined, but the components of the design were very intentional. I wanted to use the color bright, almost neon green because it is associated with mental health awareness. The bright green ribbon is one symbol that is used to promote awareness for mental health and to encourage people to engage in conversations and education around mental health. My hope in using the color green is that moving forward, every time you now see the color green, you will recognize its connection to mental health awareness and will be reminded to focus on your own mental health while also helping to promote mental health awareness to others.

Leaders, educators, and students need to be aware of what resources and supports are directly and immediately available to people on your campus. The natural first place to start is the counseling office. However, it is likely that there are more supports in place beyond your licensed school counselors. If not, I encourage you to engage your school administrative team in conversations about expanding the mental health supports available to both students and staff. With an increasing number of people experiencing mental health challenges, and decreasing school funding, schools must get creative in finding ways to provide the necessary levels of support.

I am extremely proud of my high school, school district, and community when it comes to what we have done to create an on-campus Wellness Center. Our school partnered with the Yamhill County Community Wellness Collective, which is a non-profit organization of community volunteers who are committed to creating and providing resources to community members in need. Through the Wellness Collective, they created the Wellness Center, which is an on-campus resource available to students and families. The Wellness Center is staffed during the school day with a receptionist who is available to connect with students and manage the office. We also have a designated text line that students can use to connect with the receptionist at any time. We partnered with our local hospital and university to host therapists, counselors, and interns who are able to provide on-campus therapy to students, free of charge. Additionally, students and families have access to food, transportation, and housing resources through the Wellness Center.

As a school, we realized that we were not able to provide the necessary level of mental health and basic needs support to meet the needs of our students and families. The best thing we did was to acknowledge that we needed help, and then opened the doors and created the physical space to house the Wellness Center on our campus. Looking back on it, this was a great example of a school embracing the call to *Choose To Be You*. As schools, we do not have to have all the answers. Just like it is sometimes difficult for individuals to make themselves vulnerable to ask for help, it can be challenging for schools to open up their doors to outside groups and agencies. However, if schools are not willing to engage in meaningful partnerships with community groups, we become negligent in providing students and families with the support and resources that they need. At my school, we realized that we were not mental health experts and did not have the resources available to staff the personnel needed to meet the growing needs of our students. By understanding and accepting that as our reality, we were able to engage in a beautiful partnership which has led to the creation of a highly functional and much needed space. By embracing who we are as a school and partnering with the Community Wellness Collective, we have proven that we will not let anything stand in the way of giving our students the support and access to resources they deserve. Visit them at CommunityWellnessCollective.org.

Beyond your school's counseling office, there are several other supports and resources available to students, educators, and individuals not connected to school. I am a huge fan of what the Work2BeWell.org organization is doing to create resources and tools for educators and students to access. These are completely free resources that can be downloaded and implemented into your school today! They provide access to current information and articles, have worked to design a full wellness and mental health curriculum, and are constantly creating opportunities for educators and students to engage in critical and relevant conversations.

There are several other groups and organizations working to create access to resources for those facing mental health challenges. This is not a comprehensive or all-inclusive list. I encourage you to research the local and direct resources available in your community. For serious or life-threatening emergencies, dial the emergency number in your area. For non life threatening emergency situations, here are a few options available:

NAMI.ORG

NAMI, the National Alliance on Mental Illness, is the nation's largest grassroots mental health organization dedicated to building better lives for the millions of Americans affected by mental illness. They offer numerous supports and resources.

OK2TALK.ORG

This is an online community of teens and adults who live with mental health challenges. You can connect with others who can support you and provide encouragement.

LINESFORLIFE.ORG

This 24-hour crisis line offers help and hope to individuals and their loved ones in crisis or needing confidential help for drug addiction, alcohol abuse, thoughts of suicide, and other mental health issues. The official National Suicide Prevention Hotline is 800-273-8255.

YOUTH LINE

This is the Youth division of Lines for Life. Call: 877-968-8491. Text: teen2teen to 839863

PSYCHOLOGYTODAY.COM/US/THERAPISTS

You can search for counselors and therapists in your area. You can filter your search for areas of specialty, which health insurance they accept, ratings, etc... This is actually where and how I found my current counselor, so I know it works!!!

GUT CHECK

As an **individual**, what do you do to monitor and exercise your mental health? How would you assess your current mental health? If you need help, do not hesitate to reach out to a close friend or medical professional.

As a **learner**, do you feel equipped and prepared to support your friends who might be dealing with mental health challenges? If not, what do you need in order to feel prepared? I encourage you to talk to educators at your school about creating opportunities to engage in these types of conversations and training in your own school.

As an **educator**, do you feel equipped and prepared to support students or colleagues who might be dealing with mental health challenges? Are you familiar with the supports and resources available at your school? If not, I encourage you to find out what mental health supports and resources your school has in place for students and educators to access.

[1] NAMI.org - You Are Not Alone

[2] NAMI.org - Teens and Young Adults

[3] NAMI.org - Student Guide to Mental Health

CONCLUSION

CHOOSE TO BE YOU

So… what do you want to be when you grow up?

From a very young age, we teach and train our kids that their success, value, and worth will be found, and even rooted, in the titles that they attain.

Why not start asking,

Who do you want to be when you grow up?

By simply changing the first word we completely change the narrative that accompanies the meaning and value underlining this question.

As individuals, we have the power to choose who we grow up to be. It requires us to intentionally identify and define our desired self, and then work towards becoming that person each and every day.

Life is not about what we become, but instead who we become.

They can begin to answer with *kind, compassionate, loving, inclusive, advocate, determined, hard working.* Changing our focus away from the 'What' and onto the 'Who' puts us in control of our destiny and the person we become. Regardless of what our professional title is, we should aim to always be kind. Regardless of how much money we make each year, we should be someone who can be described as hard-working. Regardless of how others treat us, we should want to be someone who others see as loving and compassionate. The power of who we become is not defined by the title on the door to our office, but by the actions we take on a daily basis that have a positive impact on those around us based on who we are at our core.

Life is full of ups and downs. Every day we meet new experiences and new challenges. Part of my journey towards mental and emotional wellness has been about learning to take each new day and new experience in stride, and to not let the impact of the new experience dictate my actions and how I choose to live my life. This is much easier said than done. For much of my life, I let the experiences around me dictate how I acted and behaved. The things outside of my control had power over my attitude and the decisions I made.

Life is not easy. Not everything is going to go the way you want it to. Things will happen to you that are outside of your control. It is important that we do not let the extremes, good or bad, impact how we choose to live our lives.

So how do you get to the point of being able to say you understand and are ready to fully embrace the call to *Choose To Be You?* Great question! It starts with learning to love yourself for who you are. When you look in the mirror, it's all about being able to look yourself in the eyes and literally tell yourself 'I Love You!' I know that sounds ridiculous, but it's the truth. When I used to look in the mirror, I could only see what I didn't like about myself. I felt shame, guilt, and disappointment for not being tall/skinny/smart/athletic/etc. enough. I got caught in the trap of comparisons, always looking at what other people had or could do, and then judging myself against that.

When we compare, we always lose.

We either view ourselves as inferior to others, which causes us to feel guilt, shame, or disappointment in ourselves in an unfair way. Or, we view ourselves as superior to others, which causes us to become prideful and arrogant, and ultimately leads to us being disrespectful towards others as we unfairly judge them through a lens that doesn't even give them a chance to begin with. When you *Choose To Be You*, you look at the person in the mirror and decide that you are going to take the talents and skills that you have to make a positive impact on the world around you. You look at yourself and you decide to commit on working on the areas of your life that need to be improved. You promise to love yourself and never give up on yourself, even when you make mistakes and experience failure. When you *Choose To Be You*, you commit to giving your best effort and to face the day with a positive attitude, because that is what is in your control.

We are constantly a work in progress. There is no end goal, no destination. Each and every day, we have the opportunity to grow and be better than we were the day before. There is no place you have to get to to begin your journey to *Choose To Be You*. Wherever you are at today, start there!

Every person needs someone in their corner, even when all the odds are stacked against them. As individuals, our friends need us to share in both their most joyful and the most difficult chapters of their lives. As educators, our students need us to be their champion and their cheering section when no one else will. Every child needs educators who tell them 'I Love You,' and who show interest in them and find value in who they are as individuals, regardless of their success and achievement. This takes an amazing amount of vulnerability, to choose to walk alongside others and to commit to not wavering in that commitment, no matter how challenging their journey might become. You are able to find strength in staying committed to who you are, which gives you the strength and resilience to love, support, and hold others accountable when they need it most.

When you *Choose To Be You*, there is no need to prove anything to anyone other than yourself. People who have found confidence and comfort in who they are at their core are not worried about what their title is, which awards they win, or how many likes they receive on social media versus their lasting legacy. People who have embraced the call to *Choose To Be You* spend their energy and effort on being the best version of themselves in each moment of every day, and are intentional about having a positive impact on the world around them, regardless of who or how many people notice. When leaders *Choose To Be You*, they become more concerned with the success of their organization and of other individuals within their organization above their own success. People who *Choose To Be You* are not scared to ask for help, and are eager to help others whenever they can. When you *Choose To Be You*, you find confidence and peace of mind in knowing that regardless of what others say or think about you, you know the truth about who you are at your core.

As educators, I believe that one of the most powerful tools and resources we can utilize in school is ourselves. Regardless of whatever technology or curriculum we have available to us, if we are not being our true and authentic self, students will recognize that. Students want to see their educators for who they are at their core, not just for who they are by the name on their door. My work as an educator completely changed the day that I allowed students to get to know Mark Brown as opposed to just Mr. Brown. Mr. Brown was cool and fun, but Mark Brown was real.

As educators, we have the opportunity to teach and model what it means to *Choose To Be You* each and every day. Instead of talking and teaching about it, start living it! It is one of the most important and valuable lessons we can share with those we serve.

If you are anything like me, the call to *Choose To Be You* will be the most rewarding and most challenging decision you will ever make. Some days are better than others and I often still find myself struggling to live my life with confidence and joy in who I am deep down, without letting the pressures of others influence my decisions, actions, and how I view myself.

E.E. Cummings said it best when he said,

"To be nobody-but-yourself — in a world which is doing its best, night and day, to make you everybody else — means to fight the hardest battle which any human being can fight; and never stop fighting."

I encourage you to spend time identifying the things that are most important to you and what you believe to be true about the world. I encourage you to reach out to people who you respect and invite them to join you on your journey to finding confidence and happiness in who you are. I encourage you to walk alongside others in supporting, loving, and holding them accountable to be the best version of themselves and that you constantly look for opportunities to have a positive impact on the world around you. My hope is that something in this book inspired, encouraged, and empowered you to *Choose To Be You.*

Every day you will have to make the intentional decision to wake up, look yourself in the mirror, and decide who you are going to be. When you make the courageous decision to live life according to who you are, and when you commit to fighting relentlessly for who you are, you give yourself the opportunity to experience life to the fullest. You give yourself the opportunity to experience a life of true happiness and joy.

"It takes courage to grow up and become who you really are."
~E.E. Cummings~

ABOUT THE AUTHOR

Mark Brown uses his life experience - the good and the bad - to help encourage, inspire, and empower others to live their best life! As a high school administrator, Mark understands the challenges facing students and educators in today's world. He draws upon his experience as a student, classroom teacher, activities director, head coach, and administrator to deliver a message of hope, perseverance, acceptance, and self-worth that inspires his audience to love themselves and others.

Mark has been recognized for his accomplishments as both an educator and a coach, being awarded Staffulty of the Month and Coach of the Year honors.

Mark is a mental health and wellness advocate. He serves as a partner with the Yamhill County Community Wellness Collective, seeking to connect students and families with resources to meet their needs. As someone who struggles with mental illness, Mark is a voice of authenticity, grace, and hope. Instead of being ashamed of his battle with anorexia, Mark uses his success and his failures to deliver an inspiring message sure to leave his audience with hope, inspiration, and applicable tools to Choose To Be You!

Mark, along with his wife Sarah and daughters Addy and Rose live in Oregon and enjoy everything that the Willamette Valley has to offer! They love spending time camping in their trailer and exploring the beautiful Northwest.

Mark desires to help students, educators, schools, and districts to embrace the Choose To Be You mentality by creating safe, inclusive, and support school cultures. He shares his story openly with anyone who will listen, hoping to encourage, inspire, and empower as many people as possible to be able to look at themselves in the mirror and say: I Choose To Be Me!

CONNECT WITH CHOOSE TO BE YOU

Mark is ready to connect with you to provide you, your team, and your school with all the tools you need in order to fully embrace the call of Choose To Be You. His programs are strategically designed so that educators and students all find meaningful and actionable takeaways. Explore the different ways that Mark can connect with your school below.

CONSULTING

Mark loves working 1 on 1 with school leaders and leadership teams to understand your situation, and then help you develop, create, and implement an action plan that will enable all educators and students in your school to be able to embrace the call of Choose To Be You.

SPEAKING

Mark uses his personal story and his struggle with mental health to engage and inspire audiences. Whether it be for educator professional development, or a power packed student assembly, Mark's presentation will leave everyone in your school inspired and equipped to embrace the call of Choose To Be You!

WORKSHOP

Mark has many years of experience as a coach and facilitator, and loves working with small groups of educators, students, or a combination of both. Mark uses his expertise as an educator and leader to work with small groups to engage them first in critical thinking exercises, but then challenging them to leave ready to not only make an impact in their own lives, but on the lives of everyone in your school!

VISIT
HEYMARKBROWN.COM
TO CONNECT WITH MARK TODAY

@HeyMarkBrown

@heymarkbrown

Mark Brown

heymarkbrown@gmail.com

MORE FROM CODEBREAKER

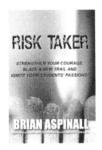

RISK TAKER

Strengthen Your Courage, Blaze A New Trail and Ignite Your Students' Passions

Code BREAKER

Increase Creativity, Remix Assessment, and Develop a Class of Coder Ninjas

BLOCK BREAKER

Building Knowledge and Amplifying Student Voice One Block at a Time

ROCK YOUR CLASS

Creatively impactful teacher rockstar tips from A to Z

STAYING GROUNDED

12 Principles for Transforming School Leader Effectiveness

ROAD TO AWESOME

EMPOWER, LEAD, CHANGE THE GAME

MORE FROM CODEBREAKER

DAILY STEM
How to Create a STEM Culture in Your Classrooms & Communities

HALLWAY CONNECTIONS
Autism and Coding

THINK LIKE A CODER
Connecting Computational Thinking to Everyday Activities

Gracie
An Innovator Doesn't Complain About The Problem.
She Solves It!

FINDING LOST SMILES
Chasing Greatness is Helping Lost Smiles Find Their Home

Scratching The Surface
An Intro to Coding in Middle School

www.codebreakedu.com

Made in the USA
Monee, IL
13 November 2020